CEZANNE

CEZANNE

FRANK ELGAR

163 illustrations
55 in colour

BOOK CLUB ASSOCIATES

LONDON

Contents

Introduction

There is a photograph of Paul Cézanne taken by Emile Bernard in February 1904. It shows an aging man of sixty-five with a lively face, a long nose ending in a bushy white moustache and a white beard which hides his chin. A few wisps of white hair stick out from under a square-crowned hat, and he is dressed in a long travelling coat which falls to below his knees. There is nothing in his appearance to distinguish him from any other middle-class citizen of Aix-en-Provence, and yet it is this thin, unremarkable old man who laid the foundations of modern painting, this very ordinary middle-class Frenchman who, in his time, was the most revolutionary of painters.

The family into which he was born, his education and the social environment in which he was brought up all contributed to make him a typical member of the French provincial middle class. His ancestors had come to Briançon in the seventeenth century from Cesana, a small village on the Italian side of the Alps at the foot of Mount Genèvre, and although many of Cézanne's biographers attribute French linguistic and ethnic origins to the family, he himself was always quick to acknowledge his transalpine ancestry, and I think that certain traits in his character can be better explained if we recognize a Piedmontese descent.

The Cézanne family made little financial headway at Briançon, and they soon had to leave the village. Since the family was a large one, it is difficult to trace their movements, but we do know that in 1650 there was a Blaise Cézanne who was a shoemaker by profession and that a Denis Cézanne settled in Aix-en-Provence in about 1700. He had many

7

1   Cézanne in the country near Aix,
shortly before his death

children, all of whom were either barbers or tailors. One of Denis's grand-children, Thomas François Xavier, baptised in 1756, left Aix to practise as a tailor about twelve miles away in Saint-Zacharie, a little market town in the Huveaume. On 28 June 1798 he had a son, Louis-Auguste, who in many ways was to be a remarkable man.

Intelligent, ambitious and hard-working, Louis-Auguste left Saint-Zacharie, where there was little future for him, to enter the employment of the Dethès, a family of Aix drapers. But he soon saw that his prospects would be better in the hat trade. Many of the neighbouring farms raised rabbits, whose skins were turned into felt by factories in the town, and here the young man found a source of income which was eventually to give a new direction to his life. In 1821, at the age of twenty-three, he went to Paris to train as a hatter, and when he returned in 1825 as a licensed craftsman, he had acquired enough capital to start, with two partners, an important business in the selling and exporting of hats.

The business opened at 55 cours Mirabeau, at the corner of the present rue Fabrot, and it was there that Louis-Auguste first began to make his fortune. A man of great vitality, which at forty showed no sign of diminishing, he fell in love with a twenty-five-year-old girl from Marseilles: Anne-Elisabeth-Honorine Aubert, the sister of one of his employees. But he was a prudent man and at first had no intention of marrying her. On 19 January 1839 she had a son, Paul, and on 4 July 1841 a daughter, Marie, and although he recognized both children from birth, he waited three years before marrying their mother. Paul Cézanne, therefore, was born illegitimate.

An economic crisis soon caused Paul's father to move from trade to finance. When the rabbit breeders were short of money, the deliveries of skins to the factories in Aix would fall behind and supplies of felt became scarce. Louis-Auguste took to granting them loans, and the interest which he received in exchange became a lively source of income. His financial operations increased so rapidly that he began to make plans to open a bank. In 1848 the Bank of Bargès went into liquidation, and he jumped at the chance. He took Cabassol, who had been the cashier of the previous company, into partnership with him. Cabassol provided the financial knowledge, Louis-Auguste the capital, and together they founded the Bank of Cézanne and Cabassol which, thanks to intelligent and careful management, soon began to prosper.

Meanwhile, in order to become a banker, Louis-Auguste had sold his hat-making business. From then on his fortune increased daily. In 1859 he was able to buy – for 80,000 gold francs (about 20 million francs in our money) – an estate of forty-five acres, the Jas de Bouffan, whose magnificent house had once belonged to the Marquis of Villars, governor of Provence in Louis XIV's day. The descendant of the impoverished émigrés from over the mountains was now as much envied by the

9

citizens of Aix as he had once been despised. They continued, however, to regard Louis-Auguste as an upstart, and found his self-assurance and shabby clothes as offensive as his success. These social prejudices almost certainly affected Cézanne's character, and Bernard Dorival remarks that 'the cause of the painter's persistent unsociability dates perhaps from his early childhood; for scratches inflicted upon youthful pride often become gaping wounds in the grown man'.

If Paul Cézanne appeared in life to be a conservative member of the French middle class, he owed it chiefly to his upbringing and education; for although his father had not been accepted by Aix society, he had adopted most of its values and intended to pass them on to his children. Paul was sent first to a school in the rue des Epinaux, then to a boarding-school and finally to the Collège Bourbon, where he completed his secondary education. He was a gifted pupil, conscientious and hard-working. He left school in 1859 with a solid grounding of knowledge and equally solid religious beliefs.

> I am going to talk without real meaning, for
> what I do always contradicts what I say. . . .
> Sometimes I throw my brushes at the ceiling,
> when the form does not follow my conception.
>
> CÉZANNE TO ZOLA, July 1860

Youth

It was at the Collège Bourbon, later renamed the Lycée Mignet, that Paul first struck up a close and long-lasting friendship with one of his fellow pupils: Emile Zola. Zola's father had died, and the boy's education rested on sacrifices made by his mother and grand-parents. His misfortunes and his weak and pensive nature deeply attracted Paul, although the other students treated him with undisguised hostility. Emile was unfortunate enough to have been born in Paris and to speak with a 'sharp accent' which irritated his supercilious school-mates, who at once made him the butt of their mockery and bullying. Paul Cézanne, older by a year and strong and quarrelsome by nature, had the temerity one day to fight against them in Emile's defence. He was to receive a good beating, and later on he told the story to Joachim Gasquet:

'At school Zola and I were taken for something out of the ordinary. I could knock up Latin verses in a trice for two sous. I was a real business-man when I was young! But Zola was an idle boy, a dreamer, a stubborn and thoughtful weakling and just the sort of person boys detest, and so for no reason at all they would send him to Coventry. And our friendship began with a beating I got one day from the whole mob, big and small alike, because I ignored their ban, transgressed their order, since I could not help speaking to him; he was a nice boy. The following day he brought me a basket of apples. "Here", he said, winking at me, "some apples for Cézanne. They have come a long way!"'

From then on Paul and Emile were inseparable. They read the same books, enjoyed the same things, and on their days off they wandered

2   Manet   *Portrait of Emile Zola*   1868

together through the outskirts of Aix, discussing their favourite poets. Soon they were joined by a third school-fellow, Baptistin Baille. Baille was a quiet boy, and his even temper acted as a counterbalance to Cézanne's excessive exuberance on the one hand, and to Zola's predisposition to worry on the other.

'It was in 1856 and I was sixteen,' wrote Emile Zola, 'we were three friends, three boys who wore their breeches out on the school benches. Every holiday, when we were able to escape from our studies, we ran wild through the countryside. Our great loves at that time were the poets, and for one year Victor Hugo held sway over us like a despot.'

The Victor Hugo cult was soon supplanted by a passion for Alfred de Musset. They even tried their hands at writing poetry, at which Paul proved the most able, as Zola readily admitted: 'Yes, my friend,' he said, 'you are more of a poet than I am. My verses are perhaps purer than yours, but certainly yours are the more poetic, the more truthful. You write from the heart, I from the head.'

At the end of the school year, Baille came out top of his class and Cézanne second. Zola, who was a class above them, carried off the second prize, and won a scholarship which took some of the financial strain off his mother. Nevertheless, as time went on, Madame Zola saw the difficulties which had begun with the premature death of her husband grow to such proportions that she decided to leave Aix. She rented a room for her son and returned to Paris. In February 1858, however, Zola also moved to Paris, and with him went the light-heartedness of youth for Cézanne. Paul, who until then had been protected from the torpor of provincial society by his passion for literature and his constant exchange of ideas with Emile, now gave himself over to the listlessness that was the chief weakness of his character. On 9 April 1858 he wrote to Zola: 'Since you left Aix, dear friend, a dark melancholy has fallen on me. Believe me, I no longer recognize myself. I am heavy, stupid and slow.'

This was the beginning of a correspondence which, owing to Cézanne's laziness, was to prove desultory and chaotic – in spite of constant urging from Zola to write regularly, for he was finding Paris unbearably lonely. At the Lycée Saint-Louis, which a scholarship enabled him to attend, Zola found it impossible to make friends with his con-descending school-fellows. He lost all enthusiasm for his work and soon found himself at the bottom of the class. Instead, he read poetry, wrote verses, and even wrote the first draft of a play.

Baille, too, had left Aix, to prepare for the entrance exam of the Ecole Polytechnique at Marseilles. Left alone, Paul turned seriously to his school work, for he had just failed his *baccalauréat* and was about to take it again. This time he passed with fairly high marks and, pressed by his father, enrolled at the Law School. The law bored and exasperated him, though not to the point of rebelling against paternal authority or fighting the inertia of provincial life. In 1859, however, he fell in love with a girl called Justine, whom he mentions in one of his letters to Zola: 'I have decided that, if she does not come to loathe me, we will come to Paris together. There we will be together and I shall become an artist!'

If at this time he felt some artistic vocation, it was certainly less strong than Emile's sense of his literary calling, a matter about which, in 1860, Zola reproached him: 'You lack will-power. You loathe effort, either in thought or in action. Your sole aim in life is to let the waters flow by you and to abandon yourself to time and chance.'

The impetuous and spontaneous child had grown into an apathetic young man, with dreams but no energy. His family and social back-ground were largely responsible for this decline in his personality, for rather than follow the example of his father, who was a hard-headed realist, with whom, moreover, Paul had little contact, he let himself fall under his mother's influence, who was a sensitive, tender and lively woman. It seems likely that she wanted her son to be an artist and that she reaffirmed, if not actually encouraged, a vocation which she had, with a mother's intuition, seen more clearly than he could. Paul had two sisters. Rose, who was born on 30 June 1854, was too young to affect the course of his life; but Marie, who had her father's authoritarian spirit and her mother's kindness, and was only two years his junior, exercised a tyrannical influence over him.

As a child Cézanne had covered his exercise books with grotesque drawings and, when he was older, he attended a course of drawing lessons given by M. Gibert, a teacher at the Ecole des Beaux Arts and curator of the Aix museum; but neither of these things meant that painting had, at first, been anything more than a game or hobby – at least not until he wrote that letter to Zola in 1859 confessing his short-lived passion for Justine. He had to wait another four years before his vocation fully emerged and became sufficiently powerful to overcome his apathy and lack of confidence, his sense of filial duty, and the principles of a young member of the middle class to whom any thought of poverty was distasteful – the poverty which was now the lot of Emile Zola.

Louis-Auguste wanted his son to be a magistrate: that would have been his supreme triumph. He could already see the most firmly closed doors of the old city being thrown open to his family, and he flattered himself in advance that he, the former trader in hats, would be greeted by even the most disdainful citizens of Aix. The idea, on the other hand, that his son might take up a profession which was synonymous with bohemianism and poverty was abhorrent to him: 'Child!' he cried. 'Think of the future. With genius you die; with money you eat.'

Having been forced to enter the Law School, Paul had just passed his first-year examinations when, in November 1859, he told his astonished father that he had no intention of continuing his studies. His father was at a loss to explain this rebellion, for until then Paul had always appeared a docile and obedient boy. His mother and his sister Marie no doubt secretly approved and supported his intentions, and Zola continued to reproach him for his weaknesses and speak glowingly of the charms of Paris, which he represented as the hub of all activity. But Paul's sudden decision had a deeper cause. Underneath his apparent lack of confidence and docility lay a violent nature, which at times broke out in sudden fits of anger and, at others, in unexpected bursts of enthusiasm and exulta-tion. To communicate, argue or exchange ideas with others was as yet beyond his patience. 'To prove something to Cézanne,' said Zola, 'is like asking the towers of Notre-Dame to dance a quadrille. He doesn't even want to talk about his ideas. He has a horror of all discussion: first, because talking tires him and, second, because he has to change his mind if his opponent is right.'

When he at last accepted the need for discussion, it was only to grumble or reply with insults or abuse. Knowing this, Zola advised him to be firm with his father but at the same time to talk to him 'gently and sensibly'. As a result, Louis-Auguste stopped being hostile and became hesitant instead. On 26 April 1860 Zola wrote to Paul: 'I received your letter a moment ago and it filled me with hope. Your father is becoming human. Be firm without being disrespectful. Remember that your future is at stake and that your success depends on it.'

Unfortunately Louis-Auguste changed his mind and Paul was forced to adopt a new approach. The struggle dragged on for another year, but at last the banker resigned himself and allowed his son to go to Paris to study painting.

CHAPTER TWO

Believe it or not, I hardly read any more. I don't
know if you will agree with me – not that that
will make me change my mind – but I am coming to believe that 'art for art's sake' is a bad
joke; but that is between ourselves.

LETTER TO ZOLA, October 1866

Apprenticeship

The two friends met again in 1861 at Zola's shabby lodgings at 11 rue
Soufflot, but Cézanne was hopelessly unprepared and his stay in Paris
was only to be brief. Zola's literary training had been methodical,
whereas Cézanne's artistic knowledge was negligible. A few works of
the Caravaggio school at the museum at Aix, copies of drawings by
Italian and Flemish masters and some old-fashioned Romantic engravings
were almost the only things he had ever seen. His only practical work
consisted of the three-year course he had taken with M. Gibert, and this
was little more than school work. At the Aix museum he had copied
some conventional nineteenth-century paintings, clumsy imitations of
the sentimental engravings and courtly scenes fashionable in Louis XV's
reign. Isolated as he was, where was he to find other models or subjects?

He copied Lancret's *Le Bal champêtre* and painted, in 1860, in a tenta-
tive mannerist style, four large panels, *The Seasons*, with which he hoped
to decorate the drawing room at the Jas de Bouffan. It is amusing to note
that he affixed to these four allegories, more out of contempt than
admiration, the spurious signature of Ingres. Later, at a time when his
own style most resembled that of the master in its classical austerity, he
wrote, 'Dominique is certainly powerful. But he is so tiresome!'

He did two further paintings, *The Judgment of Paris* and *A Poet's
Dream*, both of which are very dull; indeed, all the works of this period
are mediocre. When he arrived in Paris, Cézanne had everything to
learn. He had to improve his taste, deepen his vision and train his hand.
What he most admired at the Louvre and the Luxembourg were the

Ills. 3, 4

17

3 *Winter* *c.* 1859–62　　　　　4 *Spring* *c.* 1859–62

execrable canvases of Gérôme, Yvon, Cabanel and other similarly sterile academic painters. And Zola's taste was hardly any better. 'I must take you to the Louvre,' he said, 'and show you the work of Ary Scheffer. He is the Corneille of painting!'

Paul's father and his sister Marie had come with him to Paris, and when they left again a few days later, he went to live in the rue des Feuillantines, in the quiet district of the Panthéon. His father gave him a monthly allowance of five hundred francs; this was only just enough for him to live on and pay the fees at the Académie Suisse, where he could work from live models. But he lived in luxury compared with Zola, who was forced to do menial jobs during the day and write for most of the night. Paul worked at the Académie Suisse every morning, and in the afternoons went to the Louvre or to talk things over with a Provençal painter called Villevieille, whom he had met in Aix.

Since they were both busy, the two friends rarely met. Moreover, their friendship rested on shaky foundations, and they were bound to go their separate ways in the end. The conditions in which they lived were very different, for one was poor while the other lived in relative comfort. Their personalities, too, were incompatible. Zola was ambitious, wilful, and affectionate to the point of indiscretion; he spoke in a protective tone of voice which never failed to irritate the touchy and suspicious Cézanne, who was always quick to resist anyone he suspected of trying to 'get hold of' him. Zola was eloquent and always ready to talk, whereas Cézanne mistrusted eloquence and avoided all discussion. 'He's stiff as a poker,' wrote Zola to Baptistin Baille in June 1861, 'inflexible and difficult to handle. Nothing seems to bend him. If, by chance, he does not agree with me about something, he gets carried away, shouts at me that I don't understand and changes the subject. How can one talk to someone like that?'

Cézanne became angry at the slightest provocation. He had begun to paint his friend's portrait, and one day when Zola came to the room he had taken at 39 rue d'Enfer to pose for him, he found his friend standing in front of a torn canvas. 'I tried to touch it up, but it only got worse and worse, so now I've done it in!' Having said this, Paul tore out the pieces

5   *The Orgy* 1864–8

6   *Self-portrait*   1858–61

of canvas still left in the frame; then, turning his rage on the furniture, he began to lash out at that.

Cézanne was going through a terrible crisis at this time. Aware of his deficiencies, he was overcome by depression and self-doubt, and spoke of giving up and returning to Aix. Zola tried to stop him, but he was determined. 'Paul may have the genius of a great painter,' wrote Zola, 'but he will never have the genius to become one.' In September 1861 Cézanne went back to his family.

After his return, he had no alternative but to enter his father's bank. Paris had become hateful to him, and he tried to put it out of his mind by allowing his correspondence with Zola to lapse. But he never took any real interest in finance. His troubles in Paris receded in his memory, and he could think only of the easel and paint brushes he had renounced. In one of his account books he wrote this couplet:

> *Cézanne le banquier ne voit pas sans frémir*
> *Derrière son comptoir naître un peintre à venir.*
> 'Cézanne the banker sees not without trembling
> Behind his counter a future painter being born.'

Louis-Auguste thought he had won him back. But it was painting that had won Paul back – never to let him go. He began to attend drawing classes again, where he met up with old friends like Numa Coste, Huot and Solari. To keep his hand in, he did several landscape sketches, and painted a portrait of Zola and a self-portrait (Lecomte Collection, Paris); an old man's head and a genre painting called *Chinaman Worshipping the Sun* (formerly in the collection of Cézanne's son); and *Interior with Two Women and a Child* (Pushkin Museum, Moscow). He took the subjects for the last two works from his sister's illustrated magazines. He handled his father so well that he got him to sit for a portrait. He painted him in profile, sitting in a chair, reading a newspaper and wearing the strange peaked cap that the townspeople used to make fun of. The *Portrait of Louis-Auguste* (Pennsylvania Museum) is the least bad of the works he did in 1861; the most one can say for the rest is that they are hardly attractive. The lines are heavy, the colour has been clumsily applied in large patches, and light and shade are haphazardly contrasted; but out of these inevitable gropings the personality of the young painter at last begins to emerge.

In these experiments, nearly all the effects of academism and the worthy M. Gibert's teaching have disappeared, and we see instead the influence of Delacroix and Daumier. It is not surprising, for Cézanne's progress was somewhat haphazard, and he was conscious more of what he should avoid doing than what he should do. He was escaping from the rules and restrictions of art school. He looked and learned for himself, too suspicious to be unduly influenced, even by the old masters, always afraid of anyone trying to 'get hold of' him.

7   *Country Road*   1867

Paul and Emile still wrote to each other, but the tone of their letters was often aggrieved. 'Paris did nothing but harm to our friendship,' wrote Zola. 'Some unfortunate misunderstanding, some incident or harsh word taken in bad faith, has chilled our relationship. But it does not matter. I still call you my friend.' Yet although Paris had certainly impaired their friendship, Cézanne started to think of returning. With the help of his mother, he began to lay siege on his father, carefully avoiding a head-on clash. He might not have won him over, however, had Louis-Auguste not seen for himself that his son had absolutely no gift for finance. Furthermore, Louis-Auguste hoped that by giving him another chance in Paris he might broaden his understanding of life; so he gave his consent and granted him a reasonable allowance. In November 1862 Paul once again left for Paris.

As soon as he arrived he began to long for Aix, just as, when he first returned home, he had longed for Paris. He was always to feel like this, and divided his life between the two cities until he finally decided to settle in his home town. He rented a room in the rue de L'Est, not far from the Luxembourg, and enrolled again at the Académie Suisse. He had promised his father that he would attend lectures at the Ecole des Beaux-Arts; he duly took the entrance exam, and failed. Meanwhile he had renewed his friendship with Zola, who, since 1862, had been working for the booksellers Hachette. He had been promoted from messenger boy to the publicity department, which gave him the opportunity of meeting several well-known authors. He was as hard-working as ever and sat down each night to write stories or articles.

In the spring the two friends took to going on trips together in the countryside round Paris. Cézanne, enchanted by the romantic scenery of the Ile-de-France, made sketches in a note-book. Soon they started to take two shop-girls with them on their walks. One of them, Gabrielle-Alexandrine Melay, nicknamed Coco, behaved in an unsophisticated, almost vulgar manner, which delighted her two companions. This pleasant girl helped her aunt to run a flower shop in the Place Clichy. Cézanne fell in love with her, but he was always frightened of women and never dared express his feelings. He shaved off his beard to please her. Zola was amused by this. 'Paul has sacrificed his tufts of hair on the altar of victorious Venus,' he wrote to Valabrègue. Cézanne was as passionate as he was shy, and Coco's startling beauty must have raised a storm in him. We do not know how or where they had met, but it was he who introduced her to Zola – an introduction which was to prove important in the novelist's life. For he, too, fell in love with her. Coco, in fact, is the Gabrielle who became his mistress and later, in 1870, his wife. Although Cézanne never showed the slightest jealousy, his pride must have suffered, and this defeat must surely have contributed to the rift which eventually separated the two men.

In 1863 Napoleon III authorized the opening of the Salon des Refusés, in answer to the demands of artists whose works had been consistently and ruthlessly rejected by the official jury. Cézanne visited the exhibition with Zola and was particularly impressed by the works of Jongkind, Whistler, Pissarro, Guillaumin and Manet. He was enthusiastic

8 *The Temptation of St Anthony* 1867–9

about Manet's *Déjeuner sur l'herbe* and remarked that it was 'a kick in the pants for the pontiffs at the Institute!' He was also drawn to painters of his own age, the avant-garde of the time, who met regularly at the Café Guerbois in the Batignolles district, which had become the artistic centre of Paris. It was there that Paul and Emile made friends with Pissarro, Guillemet and the Spaniard Oller; there that they met Bazille, Fantin-Latour, Degas, Renoir, Monet, Sisley and Manet, who was the un-disputed leader of the group.

In this atmosphere of refined behaviour, Cézanne delighted in flaunting and exaggerating his own vulgarity. He seemed, whether out of pride or defiance, to want to behave like a complete peasant. Claude

25

9 *The Rape* 1867

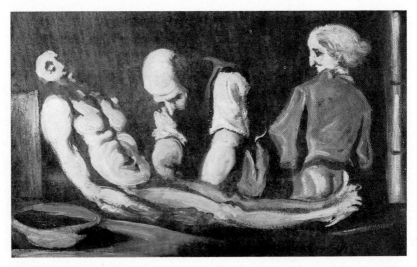

10 *The Autopsy* 1867–9

11　*The Conversation*　1870–1

Monet told the writer Marc Elder how on one occasion Cézanne had entered the café, unbuttoned his jacket, hitched up his trousers with a vulgar shake of the hips and then, stopping in front of Manet, had greeted him and told him, in a forced southern accent, that he would not shake hands because he had not washed for eight days. Manet's elegance and dignity annoyed him so much that another time, when Manet asked him what he was preparing for the next exhibition, Cézanne replied, 'a bowl of slops'.

Shy people often hide their weaknesses behind defiance or cynicism. In Cézanne's case, there was also the need to protect himself against possible influences, and the more powerful those influences were, the

12   *The Stove in the Studio*   1865–8

more justified his self-protection. The proof of this is that whereas he liked to torment anyone whose superiority he feared, he was always kind and considerate to diffident people. He did not go often to the Café Guerbois because he disliked discussions. When he did go and heard the conversation run counter to his own views, he either intervened savagely or sat quietly in a corner listening and then got up and left without a word. Zola, by contrast, was one of the pillars of these meetings; but there was also an element of calculation in his attendance. For if his fiery nature attracted him to a group of artists who were attacked by the press and spurned by the public, he had also assessed the gains to be derived from coming to their defence when he started to write for the newspapers. He was to become the spokesman for Manet and the Impressionists and bravely defended their cause, although he had too little artistic perception to understand either their aims or the problems they were grappling with.

Cézanne never really identified himself with the 'Groupe des Batignolles', as the painters and intellectuals from the Café Guerbois were now called. Degas's mordant wit, Manet's snobbery and the solemn theories and boisterous chatter of the others set his nerves on edge. The only one he really liked was the kindly and generous Pissarro. He had been resentful from youth and was unmoved by the ideas and enthusiasms of the day. He alone was unaffected by the art of the Far East, including the Japanese engravings which had just been introduced to Parisian artists by the Exposition Universelle of 1867. When at a loss for a subject, rather than seek inspiration – like Manet – in other men's work, he would go to his sisters' illustrated magazines, which had become his favourite reading. Thus his *Women in a Garden*, painted in 1870, was taken from a fashion plate, and a similar engraving gave him the idea for *Two Women Walking,* done in the same year. He still found food for his imagination in the museums, in the paintings of the Venetians and in Caravaggio, Rubens, Sebastiano del Piombo, El Greco and Delacroix. In 1864 he painted *The Orgy* (Lecomte Collection, Paris); in 1867, *The Rape* (J. Maynard Keynes Collection, London), *The Temptation of St Anthony* (Pellerin Collection, Paris) and *The Autopsy* (Lecomte

Ills. 5, 8, 9, 10

29

Collection); and in 1870, *The Idyll* (Pellerin Collection). In 1869 he painted a *Déjeuner sur l'herbe* of which only the title is taken from Manet, the elongated forms deriving from El Greco. If Delacroix's *Corner of the Studio* and *Toilette* inspired *The Stove in the Studio* (1865–8, Chester Beatty Collection, London) and his own *Toilette* (1878, Barnes Foundation, Merion), Cézanne was careful not to imitate the style of the great romantic. His own style, his own manner of painting, is precisely what we shall now examine.

Ill. 12

CHAPTER THREE

> From his youth onwards he waged war against
> the gangrene of romanticism within himself,
> but could never quite repel it. This was his
> sickness perhaps, this mistaken idea, which
> afflicted him at times like an iron bar across his
> brain.
>
> LETTER FROM ZOLA TO JOACHIM GASQUET,
> 1900

Romanticism

The source from which a painter draws his inspiration matters little so
long as he preserves intact the spontaneity and freshness of his impressions, and refuses to allow academic precepts of any kind to falsify his
vision. Cézanne would accept no preconceived rules or ready-made
solutions; right from the beginning he had been his own teacher. When
he took a canvas in hand, 'he started all painting afresh'. Such a course,
clearly, involves hesitations and risks, and the works of Cézanne that fall
into this category are no more than experiments, often abortive at that.
They demonstrate, however, what Cézanne himself called his *couillarde*
style, violent, impulsive and sensual. His drawings are contorted, his
masses lack depth, and he uses heavy materials and unpleasant colours.
His work amounts to little more than facile contrasts between light and
shade, between heavy and soft forms. An unsatisfied sexuality marks his
nudes with obscene swellings, and the breasts, bellies and buttocks of his
nymphs and Ledas are grossly exaggerated. A baroque expressionism,
stemming from the 'gangrene of romanticism' condemned by Zola,
infects his work.

Whereas the *Magdalen*, which he painted in 1868 on one of the walls   *Ill. 14*
of the drawing room at the Jas de Bouffan (it was later transferred to
canvas before being acquired by the Louvre in 1952), expresses nothing
but a sense of melancholy, the still-life of 1866, with its human skull at
the centre, shows a feeling for the dramatic. His romanticism sometimes
turned to the macabre, as in *The Autopsy* (1867, Lecomte Collection),
The Murder (1867, J. Elias Collection, Berlin), *The Rape* (1867, J.   *Ills. 9, 10*

31

Maynard Keynes Collection) and The Strangled Woman (1870, Emile Roche Collection, Paris). In his portraits and still-lifes, however, the approach is more realistic; the broad effects, the facile contrasts and that grand manner that sometimes makes one smile are less in evidence. The self-portrait of 1861 (Lecomte Collection) and that of 1865–6 (Pushkin Museum, Moscow), the four portraits of Uncle Dominic (1865–7), the one of Louis-Auguste Reading L'Evénement (1866, Lecomte Collection) and that of the dwarf Achille Emperaire (1866, Lecomte Collection), Cézanne's countryman and himself a painter, are still clumsy and look as though they had been painted with a trowel. But other portraits of the same period deserve more attention: that of the Provençal critic Valabrègue (1866, Wildenstein Collection, New York), Man Leaning on His Elbow (1867, Wildenstein Collection), Boyer with a Straw Hat (1870, Metropolitan Museum, New York) and The Negro Scipio (1865, São Paulo Museum).

Ills. 13, 15, 16

Ills. 17, 18, 22

Cézanne was now twenty-seven. Zola described him as having 'a strong head, with a beard, a fine nose ending in the bristles of his moustache, and narrow, bright eyes'. The self-portrait in the Pushkin Museum, which possesses undeniable strength of expression, confirms this description. But the Portrait of Valabrègue is a finer painting. In the naturalness of the subject's position, the impassiveness of the face and the sureness of composition, this unromanticized portrait is the forerunner of later portraits like those of Victor Chocquet and Ambroise Vollard, just as the Boy Leaning on His Elbow and Man with a Pipe develop logically out of Man Leaning on His Elbow and the Portrait of Boyer. Similarly, one could say that The Black Clock (1869–71, Niarchos Collection, Paris) anticipates all Cézanne's still-lifes, and that all his landscapes begin with Rue des Saules, Montmartre (1867–8, Renand Collection, Paris).

Ill. 19

If one compares the firm, coherent treatment of these various works with the sexual paroxysms of The Judgment of Paris or The Temptation of St Anthony, with the mad bacchanal of The Orgy or with such lugubrious compositions as The Autopsy, The Murder or The Strangled Woman, one realizes that Cézanne already had the ability to produce some very accomplished work in his romantic period. In these paintings there is

13   *Portrait of Louis-Auguste Reading 'L'Evénement'*   1866–70

14 *Sorrow* or *The Magdalen* 1864–8

15   *Portrait of Achille Emperaire*   c. 1866–70

less fluffiness, fewer patches flung on with a palette knife, fewer dark
shadows and dense backgrounds; the values are better mixed, and the
tone is lighter. The genre scenes are still all curves and enclosed in a
spherical space without depth, but some straight lines do appear in the
still-lifes and portraits. This is especially so in *Reading at Zola's House*
(Pellerin Collection), a work which is less successful than its replica *Paul*
Alexis Reading a Manuscript to Zola (1869–70, São Paulo Museum), where   *Ill. 20*
by a combination of the various planes Cézanne managed to give an idea
of depth. This painting is equally remarkable for its delicacy of touch
and clarity of tone. Two canvases done in 1869, *The Black Clock* and

16   *Uncle Dominic*   1865–7

Still-life with Kettle (The Louvre), conform to an architectural arrangement and achieve a firm basis by means of a strict interlacing of horizontal
and vertical lines.

Ill. 24   *Melting Snow at L'Estaque* (1870, Bührle Collection, Zürich) and *The
Ditch* (1871, Neue Staatsgalerie, Munich) are both violently romantic,
but in another landscape of the same period, *Fishing Village at L'Estaque*
(Pellerin Collection), the forms are contained within a narrow frame-

17   *Portrait of Boyer with a Straw Hat*   1870–1

work. Cézanne's palette is becoming richer, and he now adds browns, ochres and several vermilions to black and white. The explanation of this dichotomy in his work, this ability to pass from childishness at one moment to lucidity at the next, from overemphasis to moderation, lies in his own personality, which was likewise divided between diffidence and sensuality, between a southern need to shock and a clear understanding of his failings, between aggressiveness and defenceless innocence.

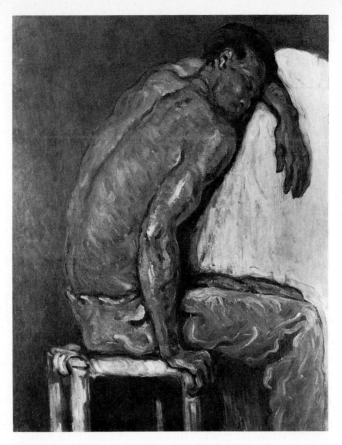

18 *Portrait of the Negro Scipio* 1865–8

Zola, who had just started to write for *L'Evénement*, Hippolyte de Villemessant's newspaper, invited his friends to dinner each Thursday. Cézanne was among the company. He would turn up unshaven and untidy, sporting a red waistcoat under an old coat that was too large for him. He seized every opportunity to interrupt the conversation, bawling out rude remarks in a voice of thunder. He would have made many enemies had it not been obvious that a sensitive nature lay beneath the rough exterior. He would call the profession of painting a dog's life, yet clearly felt overwhelming pleasure in practising it. Whenever he saw a priest, he would say angrily, 'Priests are terrible! They get you in their clutches!' Yet he confessed to his friend Demolins that he would be unable to paint if he did not believe. He could say, 'The awareness of one's own powers makes one modest,' and add in the same breath, 'You well know that there's only one painter in the world, and that's me!'

His inconsistencies are without number. Sometimes when his models undressed in front of him, he was overcome with dizziness and, when he could stand it no longer, would throw them, half-dressed, down the stairs. Then, with his skin aflame, he would return to his easel in order

19 *The Black Clock* 1869–71

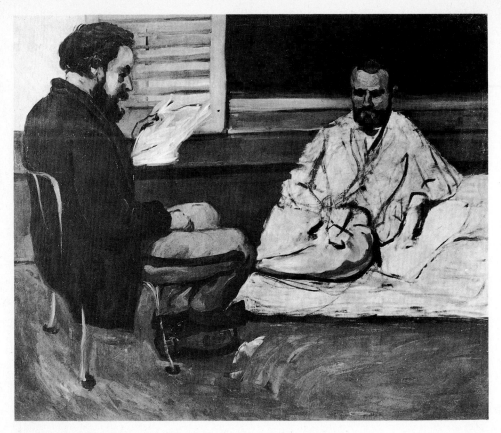

20   *Paul Alexis Reading a Manuscript to Zola*   1869–70

to 'lay them on the bed of his paintings'. The coin, however, had an
obverse side. One day Vollard began to tell him a story in front of the
maid. Cézanne interrupted him with a wave of the hand and, when the
maid had left, said, 'I stopped you because what you were saying was
unsuitable for a young girl's ears.' 'What girl?' asked Vollard. 'The
maid,' replied Cézanne. 'But she knows more than we do!' 'Perhaps,'
said Cézanne, 'but it is better to pretend that we do not know what she
knows.' To get back to the subject of his models, Cézanne had an affair
with one of them, Hortense Fiquet, which was to last all his life.

There is another explanation for the coexistence of the generally mediocre *couillarde* works and paintings which, on the whole, do credit to their creator: this was the need to defy 'those gentlemen at the Institute', and to shock the established artists and influential teachers. Like other avant-garde painters, all of whom had the greatest difficulty in getting public showings for their works, he was repeatedly turned down by the Salon, in 1863, 1864 and 1865. When this happened again in 1866, he sent a vehement protest to M. de Nieuwerkerke, director of the Beaux-Arts:

21   *Le Grog au vin* or *Afternoon in Naples*   1866–7

'I want,' he wrote, 'to appeal to the public and see my work exhibited. My demand seems to me in no way excessive, and I think that if you were to ask the other painters in my position, they would all reply that they disown the jury and want to participate, in one way or another, in an exhibition which must be unconditionally open to all serious work. Let the Salon des Refusés be reopened. Even if I am alone, I desperately want the public at least to know that I cannot stand being confused with the gentlemen of the jury any more than they, it seems, want to be confused with me.'

What Cézanne wanted was not an official intervention aimed at breaking down the jury's hostility – he had resigned himself to this fact once and for all – but simply the opportunity of showing his work to the public. He was never given the chance. The Salon des Refusés was never reopened. He continued to beat on the doors of the Salon, sending his most aggressive canvases which 'spat' at the members of the jury like so many insults, and he delighted in the thought that they made them 'blush with anger and despair'. And as if their outrageous violence were not enough, he gave them provocative titles like *The Orgy, The Rape,* *Woman with Fleas* and *Le Grog au vin,* also called *Afternoon in Naples.* He painted two other versions of this last work, which was rejected by the Salon in 1866. In the better version, a negress dressed in red raises a mauve curtain behind which a corner of blue sky may be seen through a window. She is carrying a bowl of punch to a naked couple who sprawl indecently on a bed covered in a white sheet. The woman's body is a yellowish pink, the man's brown. The wall is grey-green, the floor green.

'The model who posed for this painting,' wrote Vollard, 'was a night watchman whose wife kept a small restaurant where she served a beef broth which was much liked by her clientele of young art students. Cézanne had gained the man's confidence and asked him to pose. He complained that he had a hard grind. "But you work by night," replied Cézanne, "during the day you do nothing." The watchman protested that he slept by day. "Very well then, I'll paint you in bed!" The man immediately got under the sheets, wearing a beautiful cotton cap in honour of the painter. But since it was not worth standing on ceremony among friends, he took off the cap, threw aside the sheets and posed naked. His wife appears in the painting offering a jug of hot wine to her husband.'

Cézanne could afford to insult the members of the jury, because the allowance he received from his father gave him an independence which was the envy of other painters. At a time when there were, in effect, no galleries, art magazines or reproductions, the Salon was the only place where artists could make contact with the public. With the exception of Martin, who bought their paintings for between twenty and forty francs and sold them for almost double, practically no dealers would have anything to do with them; so painters reserved their best work for the Salon in the hope of pleasing the jury. Cézanne, however, made no concessions and never ceased inveighing against the Jury. Degas and Manet also had the financial resources to wait for better days, but the others were forced to depend upon the whim of this despised but all-powerful body. Cézanne, of course, had no intention of flattering public taste either. The new painting had a power to shock its uninformed and ill-prepared public which the blasé art-lover of today can hardly imagine. In January 1867, a dealer in Marseilles agreed to exhibit one of Cézanne's canvases, and Valabrègue wrote to Zola, 'There was a lot of noise, and crowds gathered in the street. They were stunned! There was a small show of interest, and someone asked who Paul was; but as for the others, I think that if the painting had stayed there for long they would have ended by breaking the glass and ripping up the canvas.'

At the end of the same year Valabrègue left the Midi, returned to Paris and rejoined the group of Provençals who revolved round Zola: Cézanne, the sculptor Solari, the geologist Fortuné Marion, the writer Marius Roux, a man called Chaillou and Paul Alexis, author of 'naturalist' novels, who joined them in 1869. In July 1866 the Aixois of the group, who in their school days had roamed among the hills and scrublands of Provence together, decided to recapture their youth by spending a few days away from Paris. Cézanne, Solari, Baille, Chaillou, Valabrègue, Marius Roux, Zola and his companion Gabrielle left for Dennecourt, a Norman village on the banks of the Seine, between Mantes and Rouen.

22   *Portrait of Valabrègue*   *c. 1866*

The group took rooms at Madame Gigoux's inn. They spent their time swimming, fishing, walking and talking. Only Cézanne worked. On 26 July, Zola wrote to Numa Coste that Cézanne was becoming 'more and more firmly set in the eccentric course into which his temperament forces him. At the moment he is trying to do large works, on canvases four to five metres high.' In fact, it was Zola who encouraged him to do these 'large works', because he himself aspired to do the same thing for the novel. At Dennecourt Cézanne attempted a composition with figures in it. He succeeded in persuading the peasants to pose for him, and they were so obliging that he was sorry to have to leave.

Cézanne was the only one in this period, that is between 1865 and 1872, to paint still-lifes and portraits out of a need for objectivity. There is, moreover, little difference between his portraits and his still-lifes, since both are devoid of any moral or psychological meaning. He made no effort in the *Portrait of Valabrègue* or the *Portrait of Boyer with a Straw Hat* to portray the inner life of his model. They are simply rectangles of paint. One may not agree with his *couillarde* manner, but then it was not light effects that he was after, as Bazille, Renoir and Monet were; his subjects are only excuses for balancing masses, giving density to material and arranging forms in accordance with conventional optics. He did not always succeed, but that is another matter. At all events, one cannot overemphasize the dichotomy which led him to produce such works of unbridled imagination as *The Temptation of St Anthony* and *The Rape* and, at the same time, others purged of all romanticism. In an attempt, no doubt, to account for the coexistence of works which are in fact irreconcilable, Lionello Venturi has attributed to Cézanne's clumsy and crudely expressionistic paintings qualities they do not possess. The truth is that, while Cézanne was still discovering himself, he was pulled in many directions before choosing the one best suited to his genius.

It was probably Manet who taught him the value of objectivity. Manet had shocked the Salon in 1865 with his *Olympia*, a picture which thrilled Cézanne. 'We must keep that in sight,' he said. 'It's a new step in painting. Our Renaissance begins there; it's a real painting of things. Those pinks and whites lead us along a path which our sensibilities knew nothing of before.' Here at last was an unsentimental, unidealized and honestly realistic female nude. The impact of this picture on Cézanne was such that several years later, in 1873, he painted a sort of parody of it: *A Modern Olympia* (The Louvre). He had already done an earlier *Ill. 23* version in 1870 (Lecomte Collection), and in both paintings, a naked courtesan, curled up on a bed, gazes at a seated man while a negress holds up the veil which covers her mistress. The later, and better, version has all the freshness of a sketch, but its flamboyance belongs to the baroque

23   *A Modern Olympia*   1872–3

and erotic works of the same period, such as *The Strangled Woman* (1870–2), *Venus and Cupid* (1870–3), *Le Grog au vin* (1872–3), *L'Eternel Féminin* (1875–7) and *Bacchanal* or *La Lutte d'Amour* (1875–80, Averell Harriman Collection, New York), which is a forerunner of the great *Bathers* theme which was to occupy him for such a long time.

    A Modern Olympia (second version) was included in the first Impressionist exhibition in the Boulevard des Capucines in 1874. The critics received it with sarcasm, the public with gibes. 'You remember Monsieur Manet's *Olympia*?' wrote Louis Leroy in *Le Charivari*. 'Well, that is a masterpiece compared with Monsieur Cézanne's.' And the critic of

Ills. 34, 36

46

L'Artiste wrote that 'Monsieur Cézanne seems to be nothing but a sort of jittery fool painting in delirium tremens!' Extravagant and hastily executed though it is, *A Modern Olympia* deserved better treatment than this. Moreover, Cézanne had already shown himself capable of moderating his romantic impulses. It seems to have been Pissarro who advised him, about 1869, to pay closer attention to nature and to painting that was 'faithful to its subject', and who made him aware of the advantages of simplicity, the futility of violence and the dangers of a turgid and pretentious technique.

Pissarro's advice must have seemed very attractive to Cézanne, who never could accustom himself to city life. In Paris he was like a lost soul, continually changing studio, from the right bank to the left bank and back again, continually forming relationships and breaking them again. Not being able to stay in one place, he went to Aix for the summer of 1864, returned to Paris in 1865, left again for Aix in the autumn and arrived back in Paris the following spring. This coming and going continued until the war of 1870. He took refuge in L'Estaque, near Marseilles, to escape conscription. He was not alone; the young model Hortense Fiquet, whom he had met a few months earlier and who had agreed to share his life, accompanied him. He went to L'Estaque as much to hide the affair from his father as to escape military service.

Before leaving Paris in May 1870, he had been a witness at Zola's marriage to Gabrielle. It was at L'Estaque, where Zola came to visit him for a while, that Cézanne – at last in touch with true nature – began to harness the violence of his imagination and transform uncontrolled sexuality into strictly restrained sensuousness. The baroque side of his character remained in evidence for a few more years, but the months spent on the coast of the Mediterranean were profitable ones. It is likely that at L'Estaque he was reminded of Pissarro's advice, 'Never paint with anything but the three primary colours and their immediate derivatives!' In order to paint *Melting Snow at L'Estaque* and *The Fishing Village,* he gave up the heavy impasto and black bitumens of his earlier work, and made discreet use of browns and ochres. He began to look for the right colour; his brush strokes became shorter.

24   *Melting Snow at L'Estaque*   c. 1870

When the war ended, he returned to Paris and took a flat at 5 rue de Chevreuse, next door to the sculptor Solari. Soon after he moved to the rue Jussieu in front of the Halle aux Vins, which inspired a solidly constructed painting, *La Halle aux Vins* (Lecomte Collection). It was in these new lodgings that, on 4 January 1872, Hortense Fiquet gave birth to a son, called Paul after his father. Three months later Cézanne took his family to Saint-Ouen-l'Aumône, to join Pissarro. He followed him to Pontoise, and then in 1873 settled in Auvers-sur-Oise. There was no question of returning to Aix, for, so long as he had to conceal his affair with Hortense and the birth of his son, his father's house was closed to him.

CHAPTER FOUR

Monet is the strongest of us. He's only an eye,
but, my God, what an eye!

CÉZANNE QUOTED BY VOLLARD

Impressionism

At Pontoise, Pissarro was the kindly father-figure of a group of young painters. The most important were Béliard, Guillaumin and Cézanne, whose genius Pissarro was the first to recognize. On 3 September 1872, he wrote to Guillemet: 'There is hope for Cézanne. I have seen, and have at my house, a painting of remarkable strength and vitality. If, as I hope, he stays a while at Auvers, where he is now moving, he will surprise those artists who were too quick in condemning him.' Cézanne's career now took a decisive turn, which was due partly to the advice he received and – for once – accepted from Pissarro, who used great tact in getting him to tone down the violence of his style. Pissarro believed that intimate contact with nature was the best possible discipline, and took Cézanne to work with him in the outskirts of Pontoise and Auvers. 'We were always together,' he told his son Lucien, 'but each of us kept for himself that *unique feeling* which is the only thing that matters.'

It is difficult to take this literally, for although Cézanne's personal style was not really dominated by that of the older man, he did make a copy of Pissarro's *View of Louveciennes*, in order to assimilate the painter's Impressionist technique. On the other hand, Pissarro, as he himself admitted, was as much influenced by Cézanne as Cézanne was by him; the one stressed the modelling of the shapes and their arrangement in the picture, while the other was concerned more with the colours and with loosening up the composition of his paintings.

It is striking that most of the painters who were to become famous as Impressionists left the capital, at the same time, to work in the open air.

25   *Flowers in a Delft Vase*   1873–5

Pissarro and Cézanne went to the Oise valley, Sisley to Louveciennes, Berthe Morisot to Maurecourt and Fécamp, and Monet to Argenteuil, where Renoir often went to see him. Degas had left with his brother for New Orleans. Even Manet, a town-dweller at heart, spent the summer in Berck after his trip to Holland. The Café Guerbois had lost its most distinguished customers.

At the beginning of 1873, Cézanne left Pontoise and went to live at Auvers, near Dr Gachet's beautiful house, which dominated the valley. Gerstle Mack gives us this description of Gachet: 'He was an original. He dressed in such a bizarre fashion and dyed his hair such a brilliant yellow that he was known to the neighbourhood as Doctor Saffron. His eccentricities, however, did not prevent him from having a generous and charitable nature.' He was passionately interested in avant-garde art and, since he painted occasionally himself and did engravings, he had equipped his house with a comfortable studio, which he willingly placed at the disposal of his artist friends. Cézanne did two etchings there (the only two he ever did), a portrait of Armand Guillaumin and a transposition on to copper of Guillaumin's *View over the Seine*. He also painted still-lifes of flowers and fruit which Madame Gachet had picked for him in the garden: *Flowers in a Delft Vase, Green Apples, Bunch of Yellow* *Ill. 25* *Dahlias, Dahlias* and *Glass, Jug, Knife and Fruit* – all bought by the doctor, and all but the last bequeathed by his son to the Louvre. Dr Gachet often helped Cézanne, who still received only a meagre allowance, since his father did not know that he now had a wife and child to support. Gachet also bought *A Modern Olympia*, which Cézanne is said to have painted in his presence after a heated discussion they had had about Manet.

Cézanne's financial difficulties had not escaped Pissarro's eye, and he introduced him to Tanguy, a paint merchant in the rue Clauzel in Paris. Tanguy was a strange man, plasterer, paint manufacturer and travelling salesman, as well as revolutionary. For his activities in this last capacity, he was sentenced to prison in Brest and then deported. When he was free again, he went to Paris and opened a small business. He was a disinterested champion of the Impressionists and an admirer of Seurat, Gauguin and Van Gogh. He took an immediate liking to Cézanne and supplied him

26 *Glass and Apples* 1879–82

with canvases and paint in exchange for a few paintings, which he had difficulty in selling for between forty and a hundred francs apiece. It was at his shop, which had become a meeting place for the new generation of painters, that, in 1886, Cézanne met Van Gogh.

Cézanne ran up debts everywhere. Thanks to the intervention of Dr Gachet, he managed to get his grocer in Pontoise to accept a few paintings in settlement of an unpaid bill. In consequence of Pissarro's intercession, a master at the school in Pontoise where Cézanne had sent his son agreed to buy some paintings from him. Cézanne always found support and brotherly help in Pissarro. 'He's rather like God!' he once remarked in gratitude. Pissarro, backed by Durand-Ruel, who had become the Impressionists' dealer, was now beginning to make his mark; yet he never managed to interest Durand-Ruel in Cézanne. But then nobody took Cézanne seriously, except for Pissarro and Marion – and Dr Gachet, who thought he saw a great painter in him. The concern mingled with admiration which the doctor showed him, the financial and moral support he gave him, and finally the peaceful beauty of the Auvers countryside helped to soothe his impatient, impetuous nature. His painting was no longer an outlet for repressed sensuality or uncon-

27 *The Suicide's House* 1872–3

trolled impulses. A prolonged contact with nature might have been harmful for anyone else; but for him it was an opportunity to deepen his vision, discipline his hand and put the turmoil of his sensations a little in order.

Setting up his easel in sandy country lanes, in the fields and orchards of Auvers, in front of thatched cottages, Cézanne would concentrate on covering the canvas, like Pissarro, with small touches of dry and clotted paint, which was sometimes free of oil. In this manner, in 1873, he *Ills. 27,* painted *The Suicide's House* (The Louvre), *House and Tree* (William Goetz *29, 30* Collection, Los Angeles), *Auvers, Panoramic View* (Art Institute, Chicago), *Crossroads at Auvers* (The Louvre), and *The House of Dr Gachet, Auvers* (Ryerson Collection, Chicago), of which there are two other versions, one taken from a different angle. Still under the influence of Impressionism, at the risk of destroying the forms under the play of light, he searched for atmospheric effects in *Winding Road in the Forest* *Ill. 32* (Thannhauser Collection, Lucerne), *The House of Père Lacroix* (National Gallery, Washington), and *Auvers, Seen from the Outskirts* (Joseph Stransky Collection, New York).

The landscapes which he did at Pontoise in 1875, *La Côte des Boeufs* (Hunt Henderson Collection, New Orleans), *The Mountain Path* (Galerie Neupert, Zürich), *The Hermitage at Pontoise* (Staedtisches Museum, Wuppertal) and *Winding Road* (Cazalet Collection, London), are still Impressionist but show a tendency to geometrize. In his obsessive anxiety to show depth in a new way, he returned time and again to the theme of the winding road, the most notable example being the painting in the Boston Museum of Fine Arts (1879–82). In a series of landscapes painted in 1875–6 at the Jas de Bouffan and at L'Estaque, his emphasis on straight lines had become more marked. *The Pond at Jas de Bouffan* in the collection of Dr Krels in Weimar is Impressionist, but the one in the Lecomte Collection (1878) is definitely not.

Lionello Venturi and Théodore Reff have made a comparison of the works of Cézanne and Pissarro done on similar themes. Whereas Pissarro manages to obtain balanced space by means of classical perspective and separation of tones, Cézanne, who wanted to achieve the same

28　*Pissarro on His Way to Work*　1872–6

object, fails because he stresses volume and divides up conventional perspective. The juxtaposition of two incompatible methods leads to a discontinuous, almost broken space – a difficulty which he later overcame by inventing a space and light which owed nothing to Impressionism.

Meanwhile the prestige of the Impressionists began to grow. Their work began to fetch unheard-of prices; at the beginning of 1873, a Pissarro landscape found a buyer at 950 francs, and Monet, the centre of attraction, got 1,000 to 1,500 francs from collectors. Nevertheless the jury of the Salon were as obdurate as ever. They did accept Manet's

29   *Auvers, Panoramic View*   1873–5

Bon-Bock, and the painting was a great success with the public; but they rejected the entries of Jongkind, Renoir and Eva Gonzalès. As for the other Impressionists, having decided not to make any compromises, they went in search of another way of exhibiting their work. Monet had the idea of organizing an exhibition at the group's expense. This project was received with enthusiasm, for the art market had been hit by economic depression, and the stock of unsold paintings in the Durand-Ruel warehouse went on growing. Since the collectors did not want to run the risk of depreciation, they were turning to safer talents like Corot, Courbet and the Barbizon school.

30   *The House of Dr Gachet, Auvers* 1873

31   *Crossroads at Auvers*   1873

Once the financial problem was solved – each painter agreed to contribute a tenth of his anticipated sales – they had to find a site. Nadar, the photographer, offered to lend them his studio on the Boulevard des Capucines, and then began a campaign to recruit supporters. Pissarro had great difficulty in getting them to accept Cézanne, whose work, it was thought, might shock the visitors. Manet, who had been approached by Degas, declined the invitation, saying that he would never commit himself with Cézanne. Finally, the 'First Exhibition of the Limited Company of Artists, Painters, Sculptors and Engravers' opened on 15

32   *The House of Père Lacroix, Auvers*   1873

April 1874. The public came in large numbers and voiced their disgust. They guffawed, they roared, they sneered. Admittedly, it was the works of Cézanne – *A Modern Olympia, Landscape at Auvers,* and *The Suicide's House* – which aroused most scorn. Some of the critics took a stern attitude, while others treated the whole thing as a joke. 'This type of painting doesn't make sense,' said one of the reviewers, and an article by Louis Leroy in *Le Charivari* caused a particular sensation. He spared none of the exhibitors, neither Sisley nor Pissarro nor Monet nor Renoir, and least of all Cézanne. According to John Rewald, 'Someone invented a joke to the effect that these painters' method consisted in loading a pistol with several tubes of paint and firing at a canvas, then finishing off the work with a signature.' Both the Fauves in 1905 and, later, the non-representational painters were to be described in similar terms.

The Impressionists, as they were now called after this *succès de scandale,* were not unduly worried by the insults which had just rained down on their works. It was, after all, the first time that they had been able to appeal to public opinion, and they had aroused the interest of a few art-lovers. One of these, Count Doria, even bought Cézanne's *The Suicide's House.* The jeering, however, continued. The students at the Beaux-Arts made a great clamour, and even turned on independents like Boudin, Cals and Bracquemond who had had the audacity to join forces with the Impressionists. Guichard, Berthe Morisot's former teacher, wrote a despairing letter to Berthe's mother: 'I have seen Nadar's exhibition and I want to give you my sincere impression. As soon as I entered, dear lady, my heart stood still to see your daughter's work in such corrupting company. I said to myself, "One cannot remain unscathed if one lives with fools!" Manet was right to exclude himself from this exhibition. If one examines and analyzes these works conscientiously, one finds here and there some merit, but they are all more or less boss-eyed!'

The backwash of this scandal reached the provinces. M. Gibert, curator of the Aix museum and once Cézanne's teacher, was shocked. In a letter dated 24 June 1874, Cézanne told Pissarro how he had just had a stormy discussion with his former drawing master. 'When I told him that my works would give him no real idea of how far the evil had

33 *The Garden Gate* 1872–7

gone, and that he ought to see the products of the great criminals of Paris, he replied, "Your efforts give me a very good idea of the dangers which beset painting." And when I told him that you, for instance, replace modelling by a study of colours, and tried to give him examples from nature, he closed his eyes and turned his back.'

Zola, meanwhile, was engrossed in writing his story of the Rougon-Macquarts and was too busy to defend his artist friends. He was taking less and less interest in painting; his concern now was with success, and the artists whom he had so bravely defended were taking too long to break through. Professional obligations, the necessities of life and changes in outlook were causing the group from Aix to drift apart. Cézanne had lost touch with Baille, and his offhand manner had alienated Valabrègue. Guillemet, who, in the hope of gaining acceptance at the Salon, curried favour with the jury, now found himself alone. Cézanne the painter received the catcalls and insults with equanimity, but Cézanne the man suffered under the rivalry between artists and the frivolity of Parisian morals. Moreover, his inconsistent behaviour, his unrestrained language and, it must be admitted, his liaison with Hortense hardly improved his relations with other people. Each day brought fresh cause for annoyance and, as soon as the exhibition was over, he quickly left for Aix, without taking leave of his friends or going to Pontoise to say goodbye to Pissarro as he had promised.

Surrounded by the charms of his beloved Provence, Cézanne forgot the struggles of the Impressionists, the uncertainties of Parisian life and his own disappointment. He had no intention of revealing the existence of his family to his father, whom age had made even more interfering, mean and distrustful, so he left them behind in Paris. In the joy of having found his mother again and of the work to which he now applied himself, he hardly thought about Hortense and his son, Paul. He returned to Paris in 1874, a calm, almost optimistic man, whom the Salon's continued opposition failed to perturb. It was not so for his companions in the struggle. Despite the moral victory they had gained, their first exhibition had been a fiasco. They had not only exhausted their resources, but frightened off the collectors. The allowance Paul received from his father, though small, at least kept the wolf from the door. His companions were not so lucky; however, far from losing courage, the general hostility made them even more determined.

The group had temporarily split up. Sisley had gone to work in England in the hope of finding a solution to his troubles there. Pissarro, having run out of money, had to leave Pontoise and took his family to a friend's farm at Monfoucault. Claude Monet had gone to Argenteuil, where Renoir and Manet sometimes came to paint with him. It was here that he met Gustave Caillebotte, an engineer by profession and an amateur painter, who was to become a friend and patron of the Impressionists. By the beginning of 1875 they were all in such straits that they decided, on Renoir's initiative, to organize a sale of their works at the Hôtel Drouot. This took place on 24 March, amidst an indescribable uproar. The public wanted to stop the proceedings at all costs, and their screams and threats would have developed into a brawl if the police had not intervened. Monet, Renoir, Sisley and Berthe Morisot, each of whom had sent in about twenty canvases, watched in horror while their paintings were sold for almost nothing, the bids barely covering the cost of the frames. They were forced to buy back many of their pictures. Among the buyers were the critic Théodore Duret, one of their few supporters, Gustave Caillebotte and a man hitherto unknown to them, Victor Chocquet, a young customs officer with a passionate interest in art, whose portrait Cézanne was to paint on several occasions.

Although his funds were limited, Victor Chocquet had built up a collection of Delacroixs before developing his admiration for the Impressionists. He liked Renoir most of all, and commissioned him to do a portrait of his wife; Renoir also did two portraits of Chocquet himself. He had the kind thought, moreover, to take him to Tanguy's shop and show him Cézanne's paintings, whose reputation at that time stood very low. But Chocquet took no notice of other people's opinions and followed his own taste. He unhesitatingly bought one of Cézanne's paintings at Tanguy's shop. Renoir did better still. He introduced the two men, and a friendship of real trust and understanding sprang up between them. A little later Cézanne took Chocquet to Monet's studio.

Of the three painters for whom Chocquet felt unswerving devotion and respect – Renoir, Monet and Cézanne – it was Cézanne, the most disputed of the three, whom he liked best. When his collection was sold in 1899, there were thirty-two paintings by Cézanne, eleven by Renoir, eleven by Monet, five by Manet, one by Pissarro and one by Sisley.

In 1876, Monet and his friends organized another exhibition, in the hope that it would have better luck than the first. It opened at the Durand-Ruel gallery in April. This time both the participants and the visitors were fewer. Chocquet not only lent his paintings but exhausted himself trying to whip up enthusiasm among the people he knew. The press was as disparaging as it had been three years earlier. Cézanne escaped the slaughter: he had sent nothing in, since he was busy painting landscapes for Chocquet at L'Estaque. The Impressionists' second exhibition, then, was another defeat. The members of the group fell to quarrelling among themselves, and Pissarro wrote to Cézanne describing the situation. Cézanne replied: 'Too many exhibitions in succession strikes me as a bad thing. On the other hand, the people who think that they are going to see Impressionists see only co-operatives. Hence a cooling off. . . . In conclusion, I agree with you that since some of us feel alike, let us hope that necessity will force us to act together, and that interest and success will strengthen the bond which goodwill alone has often been unable to maintain.'

This letter shows that Cézanne still considered himself wholly an Impressionist, although he no longer painted like one. Although traces of Pissarro's technique can sometimes be seen in the Auvers landscapes, he had never fully subscribed to the Impressionist creed. If he seemed at one point to have adopted it, it was only because he instinctively felt the need to free himself from his simplistic and out-of-date romanticism through some new discipline. He abandoned anecdotal painting and genre scenes, gave up painting with his palette knife, used a juxtaposition of bright colours instead of violent contrasts, avoided black, increased the number of brush strokes and went after a luminous effect, thereby developing his ambition to construct by colour. Moreover, he could not remain unaffected when all around him the winds of freedom were blowing away the old conventions. One no longer examined nature in the way that Corot, Courbet, Rousseau and Millet had done, or copied it as the academic painters had done, in the hope of gaining diplomas, medals and commissions. One looked at nature through new eyes. The work of art was from then on, in Zola's famous phrase, 'a corner of the universe seen through the personality'.

Impressionism was no more than a brief experiment for Cézanne, but it was a refining and perhaps a healthy one. It revealed tendencies in him which he did not as yet fully understand. However, a remark like 'I want to make Impressionism something solid and lasting like the art in the museums' should not be taken literally. Even the greatest artists do not always do what they set out to do; they will achieve one thing while aiming at something quite different. The same goes for other sayings of Cézanne: 'One cannot be too submissive to nature,' or 'We must redo Poussin from nature' (that is, retain elements from Poussin's more formal art while painting directly from nature). Cézanne did none of these things. He did something more important: he probed so deeply into the meaning of painting that, after him, it was impossible to be an Impressionist, still less to 'redo' Poussin.

The poor results of the exhibition of 1876 had discouraged all the Impressionists – except one, Caillebotte. Thanks to his persistence and generosity a third exhibition took place in the following year, on the second floor of a block of flats in the rue Le Peletier. Eighteen painters showed two hundred and thirty works. They included Degas, Monet, Renoir, Pissarro, Sisley, Berthe Morisot, Guillaumin, Caillebotte, and even Cézanne, who was represented by twelve paintings and three water-colours. The moment it opened, at the beginning of April, the attacks of the press began again with renewed vigour. The visitors, and there were many of them this time, looked at the pictures with disparagement; they made no attempt to understand them or the effort that had gone into them. Cézanne's works aroused the greatest scorn. Chocquet moved among the visitors, eloquent, untiring, trying to win over some of them, reprimanding others for their jokes. Théodore Duret wrote in his memoirs: 'Chocquet had become famous, and as soon as he appeared

34   *L'Eternel Féminin*   1875–7

they began to attack him on his favourite subject. He was always prepared. He could always come up with an answer where his painter friends were concerned. He was indefatigable on the subject of Cézanne, whom he placed in the front rank. . . . People used to make fun of Chocquet's enthusiasm, which they regarded as a mild form of madness.'

Cézanne found another supporter in the person of Georges Rivière, who published a pamphlet called *L'Impressioniste* while the exhibition was still on. 'I well know,' he wrote on 14 April, 'that M. Cézanne cannot have the success of the fashionable painters. Given a choice between *Les Baigneurs* and the little soldiers of the Epinal cards, people will invariably go for the latter.' To his praise of Cézanne, Rivière added an analysis of Impressionism. His arguments convinced no one. His eloquence was suspect. Nevertheless, even if the Impressionists were derided by the public and attacked by all orthodox critics, the lampoons in the newspapers, the jokes in the taverns and on the stage – all this publicity, though adverse, did at least serve to draw attention to their activities.

Cézanne was unperturbed by this new setback. On 24 August 1877 he wrote to Zola from Pontoise, where he had gone to work with Pissarro: 'I am not too upset, but the Impressionist camp seems to be in complete despair. Their pockets aren't exactly stuffed with money, and their works are rotting on the spot. We live in troubled times, and I don't know when painting will regain some of its lustre.' He was indifferent to changes of opinion, but not to his friend's problems, although their quarrels and intrigues continued to irritate him. He rarely went to the Nouvelle Athènes, the café in the Place Pigalle where they now met. He was not much missed, however. He was always rude, irritable and badly dressed, and offended the bourgeois and dandies of the Nouvelle Athènes: Manet, Degas, the engraver Guérard and the writers Paul Alexis, Villiers de l'Isle Adam and Duranty. This last wrote to Zola: 'Cézanne turned up a short while ago at the little café in the Place Pigalle, in one of those get-ups of his: blue shirt, white linen jacket covered with marks made by his brushes and other instruments, old crumpled hat. He was a hit! But such exhibitions are dangerous.' Although Cézanne revelled in this kind of behaviour, it earned him a reputation for bearishness which did him no good.

The year 1878 was even blacker for the Impressionists than 1877. Monet, Pissarro, Renoir and Sisley could find no buyers and despaired of the future. Even Cézanne failed to meet his family's needs with the small allowance his father gave him. He wanted to return to the Midi, and had the sensible idea of taking Hortense and Paul with him and settling them in Marseilles while he lived near his parents. He thus hoped to reconcile family duties with his work as a painter. His parents welcomed him home with relief, for his long stay in Paris had worried them. He left from time to time to go and paint 'faithfully from the subject' at L'Estaque or to meet Hortense and Paul. One day Louis-Auguste, who unashamedly opened all his son's correspondence, read a letter from

Victor Chocquet, at the bottom of which was a postscript sending greetings to 'Madame Cézanne and little Paul'.

Cézanne denied their existence, despite the evidence to the contrary. 'Very well,' cried his father, 'I will reduce your allowance from two hundred to one hundred francs.' Even cut by half, his allowance would have been sufficient for a bachelor's needs. This, however, was a bachelor with two dependants. To crown his misfortunes, little Paul fell ill at Marseilles. Cézanne did not have enough money and turned to Zola, begging him to use his influence to find him a job. Zola sent him money. In April the unrelenting Louis-Auguste sent the promised hundred francs. Cézanne again turned to Zola, who immediately sent off sixty francs to Hortense. For a year more, Hortense and her son lived on subsidies from Zola, whose success with *L'Assommoir* had brought in sufficient royalties for him to think of buying some property at Médan.

The friendship between Zola and Cézanne was a strange one. Although it rested on a misconception, it held fast. To Zola, Cézanne was an artist who had worn himself out by endless experimentation and searching, a failure. To Cézanne, Zola was an ambitious time-server, a professional man of letters. But each concealed his opinion from the other. There could be no understanding between the naturalistic author, who was enamoured of efficiency, greedy for success, always on the lookout for useful companions, and the shy, hesitant, unsociable painter. They did not even agree about creative work. Cézanne did not like Zola's excessive use of description and deplored the absence of psychology. Zola, who would have liked his old school friend to achieve quick success, was annoyed to see him wasting his time with dubious experiments, instead of producing a great work, solid and lasting. Posterity, however, was to confirm Cézanne's opinion of Zola's works and belie Zola's opinion of Cézanne's. But although they drifted apart, their friendship was never seriously impaired and survived the clashes which inevitably occurred between them.

Zola, completely absorbed in literature now, had lost interest in painting. The Impressionists could have done with his support. Excluded from the Salon of 1878, Cézanne with them, and rejected by the Exposition Universelle in the same year, they were so exhausted that they abandoned the idea of organizing a fourth exhibition. One did in fact take place, but not until 1879. This time Cézanne did not participate. He declined Pissarro's invitation on the grounds that he had submitted work to the Salon and it would inevitably raise difficulties if he took part in the Impressionists' exhibition. Despite Guillemet's intervention, however, the jury turned Cézanne down again. On the other hand, they admitted Manet and Renoir, a move which helped to split up the group.

Nevertheless, Impressionism was on the decline. In June 1880, in a series of four articles published in *Le Voltaire* under the title 'Le Natural-isme au Salon', Zola disowned the artists whose fearless spokesmen he had once been. He said that, although their influence was felt everywhere, they had ceased to exist. Their failure was not the fault of the public (who had been able to discern the merits of *Les Rougon-Macquart*). They had been incapable of doing great works (like his), and what significance could Impressionism have, now that Naturalism (his own) was today's universal language? 'The sad thing,' he added, 'is that none of the artists in this group has put into effect, in any strong or conclusive way, the new formula whose germ appears in the works of all of them. The formula is there, infinitely fragmented, but nowhere, not in any one of them, does one find it applied by a master. They are all precursors. The man of genius is still to be born. You can see what they want and agree with them, but you will look in vain for a masterpiece which embodies the formula. That is why the Impressionists' struggle is not yet over. They are still inferior to the works which they attempt; they stammer without being able to find the word.'

This criticism was harsh, if not unjust. The Impressionists were stunned by the blow and hesitated before retaliating. It may be assumed that Cézanne, although he disapproved, was not personally much affected. He felt no great sympathy for the painters Zola was aiming at. He had never really upheld the Impressionist doctrine. Pissarro's influ-ence on him had been only temporary and superficial. His genius drove him in a totally different direction.

35   *Portrait of Cézanne's Father*   1878–9

CHAPTER FIVE

> I am trying to render perspective by means of
> colour. There are no lines, no modelling,
> nothing but contrasts, and these are shown not
> by black and white but by the feeling of colour.
> We must show what we see, and forget about
> everything that has been done before.
>
> CÉZANNE, a reported remark

In search of a method

The years 1876 to 1880 were a period of transition during which
Cézanne's constructive tendency became detached from the Impressionist influences which had helped him to control and suppress his
violent romanticism. *The Sea at L'Estaque* (1876), in the collection of
G. Bernheim de Villiers, which was painted 'like a playing card', antedates
by three years *La Côte du Galet, Pontoise*, one of his most Impressionist   *Ill. 48*
paintings. The Impressionism of numerous bouquets of flowers which
he painted between 1873 and 1877 is more understandable, since the
delicacy and fluidity of the subject prevented him from making harsh
contrasts of planes and colours. On the other hand, his concern for
volume and spatial balance was revived in still-lifes like *Le Compotier* in
Durand-Ruel's collection, and the one in Josse Bernheim's collection,
in which the forms unfold fully in a light which has nevertheless been
minutely analyzed.

    If in the *Bacchanal* (or *La Lutte d'amour*) of 1875–6 (Lecomte Collec-
tion) the space has been over-fragmented and the rhythmic unity broken,
in the *Bacchanal* of 1879 (Averell Harriman Collection, New York),
Cézanne achieved a remarkable harmony between the fighters and the
clouds, the trees and the vibrations of the air. Although *Le Baigneur*   *Ills. 36,*
(1875–7) in the Joseph Mueller Collection, Soleure, seems to disintegrate   *43*
under the attack of violent spots of light, Cézanne's feeling for construction reappears, during this same period, in *Le Baigneur aux bras écartés* in
the Lecomte Collection. It manifests itself even more strongly in *Les*

Baigneuses (1873–7) of the Lecomte, Pellerin, Hans Mettler (St Gallen) and Barnes Foundation Collections.

This concern of Cézanne's to reconcile the moving play of light with the static nature of forms is most clearly shown in his portraits. *The Portrait of the Artist in a Cap* (1873–5, Hermitage Museum, Leningrad), with its heavily accentuated planes in the face and its paint spread out in thick, dense patches, seems to have nothing in common with the *Portrait of Victor Chocquet* (1875–7, Rothschild Collection, London), which is painted in delicate strokes of shaded reflections. Likewise the *Self-portrait* in the Lecomte Collection and the one in the Neue Staatsgalerie of Munich (1873–6) give an impression of solid masses which is absent from the various portraits of Madame Cézanne painted during the same period. In these, the plain or neutral backgrounds disappear, and in order to suggest depth the painter juxtaposes, for example in *Madame Cézanne in a Red Armchair* (1877, Museum of Fine Arts, Boston) and *Madame Cézanne Sewing* (1877, Paul Rosenberg Collection), the curve of an armchair and a blue-flowered wallpaper, thus achieving spatial cohesion and balance in spite of the hardness of the face.

He had no need to use such devices in *Madame Cézanne tête basse* (1877), which belongs to a Parisian collector. Despite its small size ($10\frac{1}{4}$ in. × $11\frac{3}{4}$ in.), this masterpiece achieves grandeur. The strength of form, the strictness of composition and the accuracy of tone could hardly be simpler, bolder or more exciting. Never before had Cézanne been artistically so successful. The two horizontal lines – one purplish red, the other blue grey – painted behind the model and contrasting with the brown stripes of the bodice, the texture of the hair, parted down the middle into two heavy dark coils, and the bent face, seen from above and painted with light strokes in pink and blue greys which drew all the light in the painting towards the face, all these reveal the work of a genius. Nothing here distracts the eye from essentials, whereas in the still-lifes it might be distracted by various details and diverse purposes. This is even more obvious in the *Bathers* series, which occupied Cézanne from 1875 right up to his death.

Ignoring the laws of natural form and anatomy, he struggled through-

Ill. 37

Ill. 38

Ills. 40–3

72

out his career to give the human body the concrete qualities of an object. He wanted to suggest the bone structure underneath the skin and integrate the nude into the landscape as an architectural element. Such courage and temerity are unique in the history of painting. He was obviously inspired by his contact with Poussin, but he was well aware that although Poussin's classical composition had been fashionable in the seventeenth century, it was no longer so in the nineteenth. Landscapes could no longer be painted like historic scenes in an old-fashioned style; what was required now was to 'redo Poussin from nature'.

This involved many difficulties and risks. Cézanne's first *Baigneuses*

36 *Bacchanal (La Lutte d'Amour)* 1875–80

were a little clumsy, and he was so aware of the fault that he soon began to strip the figures of all sensual beauty. He exaggerated their heaviness, in the style of the Flemish school, or elongated their limbs in the manner of El Greco. He now had only to arrange these bathers in a space in which the ideas of rhythm, perspective and depth, instead of being confined to illusory naturalism or direct sensory perception, were adapted to an intellectual concept of the universe. He finally found the answer to his problems by imposing the restrictions of a pyramidal composition upon his bathers. This method was merely outlined in the *Baigneuses* in the Barnes Foundation (1875–7), but was consolidated in a different version,

Ill. 40 the *Trois Baigneuses* (1879–82), which Matisse gave to the Musée du Petit Palais in Paris. In this painting, lines and colours complement each other, while the rhythm of the bodies is linked to that of the trees, which bend down until they meet the implied apex of a great triangle. He used an architectural pattern again in *Les Grandes Baigneuses,* on which he worked for the last seven years of his life.

His *Baigneuses* mark the final break with the tradition of the female nude and with all the Venuses of the past: those of the Greeks, of Botticelli, of the Venetians and of Rubens. Cézanne's nude is neither the goddess turned courtesan of the eighteenth century, nor the slave girl of Ingres' seraglios or Chassériau's tepidariums, nor Courbet's indecent lover, nor Renoir's voluptuous bather. She is closer to the *Bacchantes* that Poussin set out in a group and pre-arranged in the manner of a ballet. Cézanne saw that Poussin's work reflected some of his own aims, but he differed from him by being more realistic, less abstract and more concerned with basically pictorial truths. The famous phrase to 'redo Poussin from nature' meant for Cézanne the need to revive the classical vision and rediscover the 'virginity of the world': the world of youth, of the simple man, of the peasant, a world which was at once familiar and inaccessible. Cézanne's *Baigneuses* are no more goddesses from Olympus than they are sluts enslaved by everyday reality. The human being, which in the past had been a subject, had now become merely an object. It is treated exactly like a still-life, just as the technique used in his still-lifes does not differ greatly from that used in his landscapes.

74

37 *Portrait of Victor Chocquet* 1875–7

38   *Madame Cézanne Sewing*   c. 1877

In the *Portrait de Madame Cézanne tête basse* or the *Self-portrait* belonging to the Kunstmuseum in Bern, one is struck by an arbitrary play of perpendiculars and angles, and by the rigidity of planes which are joined with almost brutal frankness. The same applies to the still-lifes of this period, in which the painter is grappling with the sphere of a fruit, the oval of a dish, the cylinder of a glass, the horizontal lines of a table and the oblique ones of a knife, or the angles formed by the stiff folds of a table-cloth. In a systematically rectilinear landscape like the *Pond at the*

39   *Portrait of Madame Cézanne*   1879–82

Jas de Bouffan (1878) or *The Village of Cergy* (1879) on the one hand, and the interplay of straight and curved lines in *House at the Side of the Road* or *The Winding Road* (both painted between 1879 and 1882) on the other, we can see that whatever the subject, Cézanne controlled it by a geometric outline which left no room for improvisation or frivolity.

By about 1878 his work had become outstandingly original, cancelling all earlier attempts by the fact that it made a complete break with every pictorial expression used since the Renaissance. He managed to

40   *Trois Baigneuses*   1879–82

curb the sensual exaltation and exaggerated lyricism of his romantic
period, and by a tremendous effort of the will overcame the domineering
influence of the old masters. He outgrew Impressionism quickly and
drastically, blotting out all he had ever learned or seen, to discover a
vision where the material from the senses was replaced by the power of

the mind. Tireless effort led Cézanne to discover his aims and to fashion his own means while following a path which no one had trodden before him. He was a simple man in spite of his good education, self-taught through a need for independence, and suspicious to the point of distrusting the experiences of others. He was headstrong, bad-tempered, obstinate, refusing to recognize his mistakes, claiming always to be in the right. But these very faults helped him, for, by relying only on his own abilities, it was up to him to make a success of his career.

If genius is great patience, Cézanne was undoubtedly a genius. He was not blessed with brilliant gifts, flashing intuition, precocious virtuosity or any natural charm. It was thanks to his faults as much as to his virtues – to his egoism, pride, childish vanity and contempt for conformity – that he was able to run the greatest risks and yet avoid doubt and despair. When he felt the balance of his powers weakening, his courage restored it again. His uncertainties, instability and sudden moods never affected his beliefs. He always knew how to protect himself against outside temptation and formulated his own rules for action. He must have been strong to have grappled with supposedly irrefutable arguments and to have built up well-guarded positions. His works and sayings reveal a certain naïveté as well as acute lucidity, and this naïveté proved as useful to him as his powers of dissimulation. His shabby dress, his vulgar behaviour and the tartness of his language, which his natural gift for comedy allowed him to exploit, were the means whereby this weak and timid man protected his continually threatened integrity. 'You well know,' he said to Vollard, 'that there's only one painter in the world, and that's me!' But he was equally aware of his failings, and wrote: 'I deserve to be lonely, but at least no one will get hold of me . . . In life I am weak, and so I had better lean on Rome.' He was as good a catholic as he was a citizen.

However timid and faint-hearted he might have been in his dealings with people, he was shrewd and daring in overcoming his inconsistencies as an artist. After twenty years of work, research and careful thought, he had to start again from the very beginning, discard all accepted formulas and invent a new world of form and colour. He needed those twenty

41   *Groupe de Baigneurs*   1875–82

42   *Trois Baigneuses*   1872–7

43   *Un Baigneur*   1875–7

44 *Self-portrait* 1880–1

years of struggle to superimpose upon apparent reality a reality which met the demands of his own sensibility. By the end of his long apprenticeship he was certain of his aims but, struggling with his raw material on the one hand and with his own ideals on the other, he had no clear vision of the end of the road along which he was advancing with the fearlessness, but also the uncertainty, of an explorer. His ambition carried him little further than to 'redo Poussin from nature', and to 'make Impressionism something solid and lasting like the art in the museums'. He was concerned with increasing the potential of reality, thus attaining absolute truth by the subordination of nature's relative truth. But all that was still confused in his mind. It remained for his followers to pick up his initiative and follow it to its conclusion.

45   *Still-life with Fruit*   1879

Although Cézanne did not tackle the principles of painting, he at least challenged the technique. He was forty years old when, abandoning the conventional process of linear vision, he decided in favour of a spatial method based on what he called 'a slight shock'. Instead of spacing the planes out towards the horizon, he piled them up, thus achieving arbitrarily constructed depth. At the same time, he imposed an architectural order on the composition and gave colour a constructive purpose. He wanted to create volume by means of coloured planes. 'I see the planes overlapping and sometimes the lines seem to fall.' Nature offered nothing to his gaze but planes, and so he painted faces, fruit, sky and trees with square or triangular touches, which he juxtaposed in 'modulations' to depict the structure of the object. He thus invented a light which, instead of completing the design or pervading the form at the risk of destroying it, gave to the pictorial expression an intensity and solidity hitherto unknown. Cézanne achieved this through experience, perseverance and thought. Before long he had passed the stage of experiment and uncertainty, and acquired a sure and effective technique.

CHAPTER SIX

There are two things in painting, vision and
mind, and they should work in unison. As a
painter, one must try to develop them harmoniously: vision, by looking at nature;
mind, by ruling one's senses logically, thus
providing the means of expression. This is
now my aim.

CÉZANNE TO JOACHIM GASQUET

Vision and mind

In 1878, while the Impressionists were in a state of confusion, Cézanne
started another battle with his father, to whom he had not yet dared
admit his liaison with Hortense or the birth of his son. L'Estaque provided some peace and inspired him to work, but every night he went to
see his family at Marseilles. For the people of Marseilles he had nothing
but scorn: 'They have only one idea,' he said. 'Money!' Cézanne himself
was about to ask Zola for another loan when his father suddenly gave
him three hundred francs. 'Papa,' he wrote to Zola, 'is making eyes at a
delightful little maid we have at Aix.' This senile passion put Louis-
Auguste in an indulgent mood, and as a result Paul enjoyed a few months
of tranquillity. At the beginning of November, however, Hortense was
forced, for unknown reasons, to return suddenly to Paris, and since
Cézanne had already spent the three hundred francs, he had to borrow
another hundred from Zola. Hortense came back about mid-December,
and Paul began to paint again.

In March 1879 he left for Paris. The Impressionists were organizing
a fourth exhibition, but Cézanne did not take part because he had
decided to have another try at the Salon. Strangely enough he approached
Guillemet, who had now become one of those 'hard-hearted judges'
whose duty it was to accept or refuse entries. Whatever Cézanne's
motives for doing this may have been, he made no humiliating concessions to the 'messieurs des Bozarts' in any of the works he submitted.

46   *Mill on the Couleuvre at Pontoise*   1879–82

He meant to win recognition on his merits or, better still, on his originality. But despite Guillemet's enthusiastic support, his paintings were turned down. The news reached him at Melun, where, unable to tolerate Paris, he had gone to paint in peace.

In June Zola invited him to spend two weeks at Médan with him. Cézanne was surprised to find, instead of the 'rabbit hutch' Zola claimed to have bought, an ostentatious house where the novelist, surrounded by valuable furniture and expensive trinkets, lavishly entertained his friends and admirers: figures from the literary and theatrical world, publishers and newspaper editors. Zola's slightly patronizing kindness, the bourgeois luxury in which he lived and the continual comings and goings from Médan made Cézanne ill at ease. Every morning he fled from the house, the symbol of a fame he did not covet, and went out to paint in the quiet countryside by the Seine. Later he returned to Melun, where he stayed for a year, working furiously on a picture, setting it aside, taking it up again or destroying it in a rage because he thought it unsuccessful. He returned to Pontoise to work, and brought back from there several canvases: *Mill on the Couleuvre* (National Gallery, Berlin), *La Côte du Galet* (Caroll S. Tyson Collection, Philadelphia), *Poplars* (Louvre) and *House at the Side of the Road* (Wildenstein Collection, New

Ills. 46, 47, 48

47   *Poplars*   1879–82

York). In December he went to the forest of Fontainebleau and painted *Melting Snow* (formerly Michel Monet Collection). He was so completely absorbed in his work and cut off from the outside world that he was unaware of Daumier's death and only heard of the death of Duranty some time later. He knew nothing either of the scandal caused by the publication of Zola's new novel, *Nana*.

He returned to Paris in March 1880 and went to live at 32 rue de l'Ouest (in 1877 he had lived at number 67). There he painted self-portraits – notably those now in the National Gallery and the Kunst-

48 *La Côte du Galet, Pontoise* 1879–82

49   *Self-portrait*   1880–1

museum of Basle – still-lifes, and men and women bathing. For these last he used old sketches rather than engaging professional models, whose nakedness paralyzed him. Women were still a perturbing mystery to him. His shyness, his sense of inadequacy and his inability to conform alienated him from conventional society. When he went to see Zola, either at Médan or at the novelist's Paris flat, he loathed mixing with the people he met there. New faces, prim and proper people or brilliant wits scared him. Of course, Hortense was not invited to Zola's parties, and sometimes Cézanne would go merely to avoid offending his friend, who was trying to draw him out of his loneliness. He felt that Gabrielle treated

50   *The Road and the Pond*   1879–82

51   *Le Château de Médan*   1879–81

him with reserve, and it was probably to please her that in June 1879 he suggested painting her portrait. She agreed to sit for him in the garden, and he worked for several days until a chance remark of Guillemet's sent him into such a rage that he broke his brush, ripped up the canvas, to the consternation of Guillemet and Madame Zola, and fled, gesticulating wildly. His touchiness had turned a good intention into an offence. After this incident, Madame Zola was even more reluctant to see their cumbersome guest. To Zola's credit, he did not allow Cézanne's outburst to affect their relationship. Cézanne was grateful to him for this, and in April 1880 wrote, with touching humility, 'I am, gratefully, your old school friend of 1854.'

He spent four months in Paris, from January to April 1881, and they proved a bad period for him. He was again rejected by the Salon and refused to exhibit in the sixth exhibition organized by the Impressionists, from whom he felt daily more estranged. Apart from the absence of his few faithful friends, he was suffering financial difficulties. His pride was hurt by one of Duranty's posthumous writings entitled *Le Pays des arts*, in which Duranty describes a meeting between a young artist and a half-mad character called Maillobert, whom Cézanne could not fail to recognize as himself:

'"When I knocked," says Maillobert's visitor, "I heard a parrot's voice coming from inside." "Come in!" somebody shouted in an exaggerated southern accent and, as soon as I entered, I thought, "But this is a madhouse." I was astounded by both the place and the person. The painter, bald but with an enormous beard and two fang-like teeth which held his lips half open, with an air that was young and old at the same time, appeared, the presiding deity of this indescribably sordid studio. He greeted me with an expansive gesture and a smile, which could have been either bantering or foolish. At the same time, I felt petrified when I saw all those huge and hideously coloured canvases on the walls. "Ah, ah," drawled Maillobert in a nasal voice with an exaggerated Marseilles accent, "Monsieur is an art lover?" "Well," he went on, "here are the little scrapings from my palette," pointing at enormous canvases.'

Several pages in the same vein followed. Cézanne was cruelly hurt and longed to leave Paris, the Parisians and, above all, the literati. In 1881 he went to stay with his good friend Pissarro at Pontoise, and in the summer met Gauguin who was holidaying there. Gauguin felt a neophyte's passionate interest in all Cézanne's experiments. After he had returned to his desk in Paris, he wrote to Pissarro: 'Has M. Cézanne found the exact *formula* for a work acceptable to everyone? If he discovers the recipe for compressing the intense expression of all his sensations into a single procedure, try to make him talk in his sleep by giving him one of those mysterious homeopathic drugs, and come at once to Paris to share it with us.' According to John Rewald, Cézanne, nervous and suspicious as ever, 'did not take this pleasantry too well and seriously began to fear that Gauguin was out to "steal" his sensations.' From then on, Cézanne made no attempt to conceal his dislike for the future theorist of 'Synthetism' and told Emile Bernard: 'He never understood me. I have never wanted to achieve, nor will ever approve of, lack of modelling and gradation. It's nonsense! Gauguin's not a painter. He produces nothing but Chinese pictures!' Cézanne, in fact, despised all his contemporaries with the exception of Monet, Renoir and Pissarro, this last being the only one whose advice he accepted. 'He was a father to me,' he said, 'a man you could ask about anything, like God!'

His stay at Pontoise was peaceful and rewarding. Whereas Pissarro would soften outlines in a painting and try to work by 'no matter what method and with no concern for craftsmanship' in order to find the 'spot of colour exactly right in tone and value', Cézanne would apply a totally opposed conception and method, as may be seen in *Poplars, Mill on the Couleuvre* and *La Côte du Galet*. It shows how little he cared for other people's work, even that of the artist he most respected. He left Pontoise in October and, after a visit to Médan, hurriedly left again for Provence. At the end of January 1882, he was in Marseilles when Renoir, just back from a long tour of Italy, asked whether he could meet him. Cézanne was delighted and persuaded Renoir to accompany him to L'Estaque. Renoir was so struck by the beauty of the place and its Mediterranean light that he delayed his return to Paris. He wrote to Madame Charpentier: 'I have perpetual sunlight, and I can rub out and begin again as often as I like; that is the only way to learn. In Paris you have to be content with so little.' Unfortunately, Renoir fell ill with pneumonia. Panic-stricken, Cézanne asked his mother to come, and together they nursed Renoir with a devotion and selflessness that he was always to remember. This picture of Cézanne is the antithesis of Duranty's caricature.

That same year Cézanne was admitted to the Salon for the first time. He owed this 'honour' to a ruse of Guillemet's, who had used a jury

52   *The Little Bridge at Maincy*   *c.* 1882–5

member's right to rescue a work by one of his pupils. Consequently Cézanne's name in the catalogue was followed by the words 'Pupil of Antoine Guillemet'. To have been accepted out of charity was too much for him, and he wondered whether no one was on his side. He went to see Zola. But the 'Master of Médan', who in thirty years had never failed him, was becoming more important, more revered each day and presented an overbearing picture of success. There was no place for Cézanne in a world open only to the rapacious or the sycophantic. He had no alternative but to give up Paris, Médan and all the hopes which

94

had involved him in so many exhausting struggles. 'All I deserve,' he sighed, 'is loneliness.'

In October he returned to the Jas de Bouffan, intending never to leave it again. He rejoined his autocratic father, his quiet, gentle mother, his severe sister Marie and his younger sister Rose, who had come to the Jas to give birth to her child. He felt almost like an intruder in his own family and stayed in his room or wandered about the countryside in search of inspiration. In Aix he avoided the people he knew and, when he met one of his old school friends, he pretended not to have seen him. No one really wanted to know the shabbily dressed failure from Paris. At forty-three, Cézanne felt worn out and on the verge of collapse. He heard that one of his friends, Marguery, had killed himself a few months earlier by jumping out of a window of the Palais de Justice, and news came from Paris that Manet was gravely ill. He became haunted by the idea of death and decided to make his will. Since he had no idea how to set about it, he asked Zola's advice. He did not want his sisters to inherit anything if he died, and he asked Zola what legal formula would ensure that the inheritance would pass to his mother and his child. We do not know what Zola replied, but in any case Cézanne did not pursue the matter further, for the desire to work had gripped him again. He went out to paint in the countryside round Aix and at L'Estaque, making only brief visits to the Jas de Bouffan, where his sister Marie was pressing him to marry Hortense.

Edouard Manet died on 30 April 1883. It is doubtful whether Cézanne went to the funeral on 3 May, as John Rewald claims, for it does not seem likely that he would have been willing to go to Paris to pay his respects to a painter whom he had admired but disliked. Furthermore, he again became enraptured by the charms of his beloved Provence. Never before had he felt so close to it, with its harsh blocks of stone, impenetrable masses of vegetation and the almost cubic shapes of the red-roofed houses contrasting with the undulation of the earth which had been warmed for centuries by the generous rays of the sun. He made friends with the Marseilles painter Monticelli, who was as careless about his behaviour and as lonely as Cézanne, and who accompanied him on his wanderings between Aix and Marseilles. The talkative and cheerful sixty-year-old bohemian was a great comfort to Cézanne. While Cézanne painted, Monticelli took notes, for he could work only in his room – with the windows covered by a red curtain during the day, or by the trembling light of several candles at night. Monticelli worked in this bizarre setting on his clever colour combinations and mysterious mixtures of materials. The two artists got on well together, especially as neither tried to impress his ideas on the other.

53   *The Bay of Marseilles Seen from L'Estaque*   1883–5

54   *The Bay of Marseilles Seen from L'Estaque*   1883–5

After a time, Cézanne became exhausted by his cross-country walks and the journey between Aix and Marseilles, and settled in L'Estaque with his wife and son, 'in a little house with a garden just below the station', at the foot of a rocky, pine-covered slope. In front of the house the red roofs of the village stretched down towards the blue waters of the bay, bounded in the distance by the island of Maire and the mountains of Marseilleveyre. Cézanne often paid tribute to the place in his paintings and letters. He had written to Pissarro on 2 July 1876: 'It's like a playing card, with red roofs over a blue sea. The vegetation does not change: evergreen olive trees and pines.'

Cézanne had shown a disposition for the permanence of things even

before his Impressionist period. No painter before him had constructed
a seascape in such a firm style, and no one had purged it so ruthlessly of
detail in order to pare it down to a sequence of masses and planes. This
is borne out by the various paintings he did at L'Estaque in 1883 and
1884 which are now in the Louvre, the Metropolitan Museum, the
Pellerin Collection, the Dresden Museum and the Courtauld Institute;
by those in the collections of Paul Mellon (Washington), Adolph
Lewisohn (New York) and Stirling (Zürich); and, above all, by the

55   *Rocks at L'Estaque*   1882–5

Rocks at L'Estaque in the museum of São Paulo, an incomparable work, *Ill. 55*
in which the artist's sharp eye seems to have penetrated the earth's surface
to the core. Imagine how an Impressionist would have approached the
same subject, assuming that he were attracted to a landscape where a
cloudless sun accentuates clear features and sharp outlines. When Monet
and Renoir went to L'Estaque in 1883, it was to see Cézanne, not to look
for inspiration. There were no light breezes in the air, no reflections or
wavelets on the sea stretching out like a sheet of polished steel, but only
a burning light which, far from softening form with its momentary
pulsations, threw all outlines into sharp relief.

This exactly suited Cézanne's deepest aspirations. These were the
natural elements which he translated into a calm but intensely concentrated vision and which he transformed into pure plastic shapes. In his
paintings of L'Estaque, the rock and plant masses, the cubic houses, the
vertical lines of the chimneys and bell-towers and the flat spaces of the
sky and sea are united with great care to create rhythms, relations and
harmonies whose strength of expression is further increased by an
emotional perspective which replaces classical perspective with remarkable daring. Cézanne did not hesitate to raise the horizon sharply until
the sea almost filled the sky, and to arrange the red roofs in rigid parallels
without bothering about disappearing lines. For decorative purposes,
he framed his landscapes within columns of trees and gave the colours
in the background as much, if not more, intensity as those in the
foreground.

Similar aims are discernible in the still-lifes of this period: *Vase of
Flowers with Apples* (J. Laroche Collection, Paris), *Still-life with Soup* *Ills. 56,*
Tureen (Louvre) and *The Chest of Drawers* (Neue Staatsgalerie, Munich). *57*
They became increasingly important to him in the years that followed:
he was indifferent to the transient effects of light, and became more and
more involved with the idea of the stability, permanence and solidity of
the coloured form. He soon began to remove those elements which he
considered too changeable or fluid, like the sea, which he pressed
between the two arms of the bay, or the sky, which he pushed as far as
possible towards the upper edge of the canvas, or to which he gave the

solidity of a mass. From 1885 onwards, the landscapes of L'Estaque, the Jas de Bouffan and Gardanne are controlled by a rigidly geometric method, which the Cubists were to adopt, and exploit to the full, twenty-five years later. Cézanne's pictures of L'Estaque were so original, and altered the concept and technique of painting so radically, that many painters – Braque, Dufy, Derain, Marquet, Camoin – came to L'Estaque to follow in his steps.

Monticelli, whose health was now impaired, had lost his cheerfulness and never left Marseilles. Cézanne, having lost a companion, was unable to replace him, even from among the friends of his youth. He sought solitude to paint, but never rejected anyone who showed him understanding. When Valabrègue, on his own initiative, came to see him, Cézanne was overjoyed. Valabrègue wrote to Zola from Aix in February 1884: 'We walked around the town together and reminisced about the people we had known. But how different our feelings are!'

Nobody understood Cézanne or his work. His father, mother and sisters were kind to him in a way which exasperated him. 'If only my family were indifferent,' he wrote to Zola on 25 April 1885, 'all would be well.' Hortense grumbled continually about Provence, where she felt an outsider, and found many reasons for returning to Paris for good. Nothing interested her. 'My wife likes nothing but Switzerland and lemonade,' Cézanne told Vollard. Admittedly, she agreed to sit for Cézanne for hours, but only to avoid a quarrel.

In May 1885, he became the sad protagonist in a love affair about which we have few details. At the Jas de Bouffan there was a maid called Fanny, a strong, attractive girl with whom Cézanne fell in love, but in such a childishly clumsy way that the whole family realized it. Louis-Auguste, eighty-seven years old and growing feeble, had given the reins of the household to Marie, and it was she who now tried to restore order in the family. She begged her brother to be reasonable and marry Hortense. Cézanne cowered under the storm but would not give in. It seems likely that Fanny was dismissed, and that in his bewilderment Cézanne decided to write to her. On 14 May he begged Zola to help:

'I am writing to you so that you will have to reply. I want you to do

56   *The Chest of Drawers*   1883–7

something for me – trivial for you but tremendously important for me. This is, to accept letters addressed to me and post them to an address which I will send you later. I am either mad or sane. *Trahit sua quemque voluptas!* I have need of you and I beg you to forgive me. Happy are the wise! Don't deny me your help. I don't know where to turn.'

The incoherence of this letter shows how distraught his thwarted love had made him. The indefatigable Marie, however, continued to harass him with reprimands and reproaches, and he, for his part, continued to resist. Life at the Jas de Bouffan soon became unbearable.

57   *Still-life with Soup Tureen*   1883–5

Finally, Cézanne, exhausted by the struggle, fled and picked up Hortense and Paul in Marseilles to take refuge with Renoir at La Roche-Guyon. He tried to work there, but his heart was not in it. On 11 July, one month after his arrival at Renoir's, he left for Villennes, the nearest town to Médan, Zola being unable to have him to stay because Gabrielle was ill. It was impossible to find accommodation at Villennes, so he went back down the Seine to Vernon, where he booked in at a hotel and scribbled a note to Zola. The days passed in anxious waiting for news which was slow to come. Cézanne was impatient, for it was three years since he had last seen the friend to whom he always turned when most lonely. At last, on 22 July, he received an invitation to go and see Zola. But the meeting was not as pleasant as he had anticipated, and a certain unease separated the two men. Zola was now accustomed to large editions, fame and wealth. New acquisitions and successive renovations had transformed Médan into a huge and ostentatious house, which made an unpleasant impression upon Cézanne. A peasant, failed artist, and the sad hero of

58   *The Kitchen Table*   1888–90

below-stairs romances, that is how Cézanne must have appeared to Zola whenever he glanced down at him from the pinnacle of his fame. Zola was then working on *L'Oeuvre*, the fourth volume of his *Rougon-Macquart*. Its theme was the drama of artistic creation, an imposing subject which Balzac had already dealt with in *Le Chef-d'oeuvre inconnu*. *L'Oeuvre* was also a realistic novel, concerning a certain Claude Lantier, and Claude Lantier was none other than Cézanne. We may be sure that if Zola read out to him any pages from his manuscript, he chose those which would not dismay his listener.

Cézanne cut short his stay in Médan, on one of his habitual impulses, and returned suddenly to Aix. Every morning, with his materials on his back, he went to Gardanne, where he had found lodgings for Hortense. It was a picturesque town, some six miles from the Jas de Bouffan, and he loved to paint its windmills and houses, which were either perched on the hillsides or scattered over the plain, with Mont Sainte-Victoire in the distance. He delighted in completely encircling their masses, underlining their volume and arranging them like cubes in a rigidly structured composition. Over the whole fell a harsh light, without gradations, outlining shapes and sharpening the red roofs and blue shadows.

It has been said that the beginning of Cubism lies in the landscapes of Gardanne, and certainly the *Village of Gardanne* (Hirschland Collection, Harrison, N.Y.), for instance, is very close to Braque's *House at L'Estaque* or Picasso's *Houses on the Hillside,* two early Cubist works. The other *Ills. 59, 60* Gardanne landscapes – notably those of the Barnes Foundation (Merion) and of the Charles A. Loeser (Washington), Harriman (New York) and Oppenheim (Berlin) Collections – as well as the *Jas de Bouffan* (National Gallery, Prague) of the same period (1885–6) illustrate what Cézanne was to write in his famous letter to Emile Bernard of 15 April 1904: 'To see in nature the cylinder, the sphere, the cone, the whole being set into perspective so that each side of an object or plane converges on a central point. Lines running parallel to the horizon create distance . . . The lines perpendicular to that horizon create depth.' In her book *Cézanne et l'expression de l'espace,* Mme Liliane Brion-Guerry rightly observes that this letter to Emile Bernard, which is the best explanation of Cézanne's spatial method, expresses an idea which was no longer that of the painter at the time of writing the letter.

In the views of Gardanne, more than those of L'Estaque, the construction became a purely intellectual creation, with no immediate connection with the material of nature. Reality is present, but it has been transformed by imagination and intellectual speculations. Cézanne was obsessed with his vision of the geometric structure beneath the surface of things. Anything which distracted him from this exasperated him: his sister Marie's continual recriminations, the duties as son, brother and father which kept him torn between two families who ignored each other, the strain of travelling constantly between the Jas de Bouffan and Gardanne and the fatigue which resulted. He decided at last to rent a flat in a house just below old Gardanne, and settled there with Hortense and Paul. He was now forty-six and, although in his prime, felt physically weak. He did not, however, give up his long cross-country walks, which often kept him away from home. He ate in a farm, slept in a barn and returned to Gardanne exhausted but filled with new experiences. He bought a donkey to carry his personal possessions and painting materials and had to put up with its stubbornness and unpredictable moods.

He even worked when the weather was bad, painting a vase of flowers, fruit, a jug, a crumpled table-cloth or portraits of himself, Hortense and Paul. The remarkable fact about these portraits is that they are unconcerned with any psychological interpretation of the sitter; Cézanne was wholly intent on expressing form by means of colour. Two portraits of his son – one head and shoulders only (Walter Collection, Paris), the other half-length (National Gallery, Washington) – are painted with great delicacy, to be found again in the portraits of Hortense also painted about 1885, now in the collections of S. S. White (Ardmore, USA), H. P. MacIlhenny (Philadelphia), Walter and Matisse. The self-portraits are stronger and more realistic: although *Cézanne au chapeau melon* (G. Bernheim de Villers Collection, Paris) exhibits in the lip movements and vitality of expression an intense inner life, the *Self-portrait with Palette* (formerly in the collection of Cézanne's son) is almost

Ill. 61

59   *View of Gardanne*   1885–6

60 *Jas de Bouffan* 1885–7

impersonal. The light throws on the face a mosaic of geometric strokes, while the purplish jacket, the bluish background behind the sitter, the frame which cuts obliquely across the right-hand side of the picture and the palette in his hand are all painted with wide and nervous strokes. Cézanne seems to be as indifferent to human unrest and tides of change as are the blue vase, emerald green jug, ochre table and orange-yellow apples in his still-lifes, or the stones of the Gardanne houses and the rocks of Mont Sainte-Victoire, which for centuries have thrust their jagged shapes into the dry air of Provence.

61   *Self-portrait with Palette*   1885–7

CHAPTER SEVEN

I ran into a friend who told me that he had
heard someone ask Zola, 'Are you going to
eat at Cézanne's?', and that Zola had replied,
'Why go to see that failure again?'

CÉZANNE QUOTED BY VOLLARD

Cézanne and Zola: end of a friendship

Since Cézanne was completely absorbed in his work, with hardly any
free time, it is unlikely that he had heard about Zola's novel *L'Oeuvre*,
which was serialized in *Gil Blas* from December 1885 onwards, before
it appeared in book form. The rumour that the book described real
characters at once spread through Paris. The Impressionists were thrown
into a state of agitation, for it was at them that Zola aimed the unflattering
remarks with which he had sprinkled his book: 'They are content with
sketches and fleeting impressions; not one of them seems to have the
strength to become the master we expected.' Claude Monet wrote to
Zola: 'You have carefully ensured that none of your characters looks
like any one of us, but I am afraid that our enemies among the press and
the public will nevertheless talk of Manet, or at least of my own friends,
and make failures of them, which I refuse to believe is your intention.'

The readers of *L'Oeuvre* took great pleasure, not without a touch of
malice, in finding out the real identity of the characters described. It was
not difficult to see Solari in Mahondeau, Guillemet in Fagerolles, and
Cabanel in Mazel. Dubuche seemed to be Baille; Sandoz, Zola himself.
Some thought that Claude Lantier, the hero of the book, was Manet but
Cézanne knew better. Lantier, who 'was never content, who could not
bear his inability to give birth to his genius', was undoubtedly Cézanne.
There were too many personal details about the three friends for it to be
otherwise: their companions at school, their teachers at the Collège
Bourbon, their bathing parties in the Arc, their walks in the Aix country-
side, their favourite books, Cézanne and Baille's arrival in Paris, Thurs-

day evenings at Zola's and their meetings in the Café Guerbois. They were all there, despite stylistic attempts to disguise them. No one could fail to recognize Cézanne in Claude Lantier, the painter 'whose unbridled genius left the talents of others far behind', or who, 'mad with work', gave vent to his frustration by 'lashing out at the furniture'. Zola could have been thinking of no one else when he wrote, 'It was a continual struggle, ten hours a day and complete self-sacrifice – and then, after twenty years of dedication, he achieved so little. So many hopes and sufferings, a lifetime spent in the hard labour of creation, and then this, this, was the result!'

Each word struck Cézanne cruelly. It mortally wounded his pride and self-respect to see himself in this puppet, this madman, this dauber whose failure ends in suicide by hanging. Yet even more unbearable was the pity and contempt with which Zola spoke of a friend he had known for thirty years. During all that time, then, he had never once been understood. But had he understood Zola any better? *L'Oeuvre* proves that Zola was very fond of him, and the novel was not really intended to hurt or ridicule him. Zola's behaviour may be attributed to literary egoism. After all, what Zola really failed to understand was not so much Cézanne as painting in general. The theorist of naturalism and supposedly scrupulous observer of society and its morals failed to distinguish between an artist's genius and his actions, or between his destiny as a man and his destiny as an artist.

Perhaps Cézanne had intuitively realized this misunderstanding for, even after their friendship had broken up, there was something ambiguous about their relationship. Once, when someone was discussing Zola, Cézanne blurted out, 'Zola was a second-rate mind and a hateful friend! He saw no one but himself. *L'Oeuvre*, in which he means to describe me, is nothing but a disgusting distortion, a lie designed to achieve his own glory.' And he confessed to Vollard that 'there was never any quarrel between us. It was I who first stopped seeing him. He'd become a filthy bourgeois.' When, in October 1902, he learned of Zola's death, he was beside himself with grief, and in May 1906, at the unveiling of Zola's bust at the Bibliothèque Méjanes, he burst into tears when he heard

Numa Coste's tribute to the novelist. Zola, for his part, never said a word against his friend. 'My dear, great Cézanne,' he continued to call him.

On 4 April 1886, Cézanne wrote the following short note to Zola from Gardanne; it was the last he ever sent him:

'My Dear Emile, I have just received *L'Oeuvre*, which you were kind enough to send me. I thank the author of *Les Rougon-Macquart* for this token of remembrance, and I beg him to allow me to shake his hand to commemorate past years. Yours ever, in memory of the old days.' Zola was astounded. A few days later Gabrielle removed Cézanne's paintings

62 *House on the Banks of the Marne*   1888–90

from the rooms at Médan and took them up to the attic. The rupture was complete.

After the publication of *L'Oeuvre*, Monet, Pissarro and Renoir also broke with Zola, who seemed no longer to have anything in common with them. Cézanne's estrangement from Zola increased his distrust of literature and literati, and he often mentioned the dangers of becoming involved with them, especially in his letters to Emile Bernard. To Joachim Gasquet he wrote: 'The wrong that Proudhon did to Courbet, Zola would have done to me.' On 28 April 1886, shortly after his farewell letter to Zola, he married Hortense Fiquet at Aix after Marie had obtained his parents' consent. Hortense and her son immediately went to live at the Jas de Bouffan. Six months later Louis-Auguste died, at the age of eighty-eight, leaving his son a legacy which meant that he would be comfortably off for the rest of his life. 'My father,' he said, 'was a man of genius, he left me an income of twenty-five thousand francs.' This stroke of luck, however, did not alter his way of life, which justified Zola's reproach that he was indifferent to public opinion. 'He despises all basic things: hygiene, good behaviour and polite language.'

Hortense, who was bored at the Jas de Bouffan and had to supervise the education of their fifteen-year-old son, lived most of the time in Paris. Cézanne was not sorry; he seemed to enjoy the peaceful life with the family, the company of his beloved mother and of his sister Marie, who ran the house with a firm and able hand. He had lost touch with his friends: Pissarro, Renoir, Chocquet and Tanguy were too far away in Paris. So nothing distracted him from his sole concern, his work, 'the only retreat in which one finds contentment'. He was unaware, in his seclusion, that he was becoming famous, for although he was still abused by the press and unknown to the public, a few connoisseurs were showing interest in him. Not only Duret and Chocquet bought his paintings but also artists, such as Manet, Pissarro, Gauguin and the young Signac. Beginners like Louis Anquetin and Emile Bernard were enthusiastic about the Cézannes which Tanguy showed them; and so possibly was Van Gogh, who, according to some sources, met Cézanne at dinner at Tanguy's house in the rue Clauzel. However, there is no reliable evidence to corroborate this story. In the middle of the hypothetical meal, Cézanne is alleged to have said to Van Gogh, 'Really, you paint like a madman!' But this offensive remark is not in keeping with what we know of Cézanne's character; furthermore the Van Gogh of the Parisian period was not mad, nor was he yet an inmate of the Saint-Rémy asylum. Cézanne did go to Paris in 1886, but whether he met Van Gogh is uncertain. Before returning to the Midi, he went to see Chocquet at Hattenville in Normandy and painted a new portrait of him, completely different from the three portraits he had done in 1876, 1877 and 1879 under the influence of Impressionism.

In spring 1887, the group known as Les Vingt, in Brussels, invited him to exhibit alongside Pissarro and Seurat. Although the year had been one of misery and anxiety – the death of his father following on his estrangement from Zola, the poor state of his health and the complaints of Hortense, who had no intention of ever leaving Paris – it was one of the most productive years of his career. At the beginning of 1886, he returned to Paris and rented a flat at 15 quai d'Anjou, on the Ile Saint-Louis, a quarter already very popular among artists. But he grew restless. Since he was no longer restrained by lack of money, he gave in to his mood and moved to the rue du Val-de-Grâce. He either went to the Louvre or worked in the open air in the environs of Paris. He painted *Le Pont sur la Marne à Créteil* (Pushkin Museum, Moscow), *Dovecot at Bellevue* (Museum of Art, Cleveland) and *House on the Banks of the Marne* (National Gallery, Washington), in which his concern for volume is very apparent. He moved again, to a *pension* in Chantilly, and was so attracted by the forest that he went there almost every day to draw and paint in watercolour or oils. When he returned to Paris five months later, he brought back with him one of his most striking landscapes, the *Road at Chantilly* (Chester Beatty Collection, London), in which the structural element is very strong. It was at this date that trees began to excite his imagination. The subject recurs in 1890, in *Chestnut Trees at the Jas de Bouffan* (formerly G. Bernheim de Villers Collection, Paris) and in the various paintings inspired by the Château Noir park towards the end of his life. In the latter, a great lyric breeze shakes the trees and leaves, but

Ills. 62, 63

63   *Dovecot at Bellevue*   1888–92

in the former the confused mass of vegetation is controlled by the
intellect, which transforms the mingled masses of trunks, branches,
foliage and gaps of light into clearly outlined and rigidly joined planes.

Ills. 68,   In Paris, in 1888, he painted two of his most famous works: *Harlequin*
69   (Rothschild Collection, London) and *Mardi-Gras* (Pushkin Museum,
Moscow). Since few models would put up with his fussy demands, he
inflicted the discomfort of posing for *Harlequin* on his son Paul. Dressed
in a blue-and-red check costume, he is painted standing, with his right
leg disproportionately elongated. This distortion was essential for the

114

64   *Road at Chantilly*   1888

powerful effect at which Cézanne was aiming. The same Harlequin reappears in *Mardi-Gras*, preceded by a Pierrot for which a young friend of Paul's, Louis Guillaume, had posed. The juxtaposition, as if pasted on, of the Harlequin and the Pierrot in this picture, which has been deliberately stripped of grace and flexibility, recalls the artless seriousness of an Epinal. The distortion of form, the vitality of colour and the novelty of the spatial order give these two works such originality that the Fauves and Cubists became obsessed by them. Cézanne's Harlequin and Pierrot gave rise to a complete iconography which Picasso, Derain, Juan Gris and Rouault each interpreted in his own way.

65   *Mountains in Provence*   1886–90

66 *Little Paul*

According to some biographers, 1888 marked the end of Cézanne's 'constructive' period and the beginning of his 'synthetic' one (1888–95). This division, however, fails to take into account the permanent values which give his work its unity. After the inevitable hesitations at the beginning of his career, he was always true to his ideal, which was to create a real painting, whose shapes and colours would form an autonomous and absolute whole, free from caprice, fashion or contamination by anecdotal painting or literature. It is in this sense that one must take his much-quoted and often misunderstood saying, 'I want to make Impressionism something solid and lasting like the art in the museums.'

After Impressionism had taught him that light is the chief generator of colour, he discovered that light is likewise the main basis for balance and harmony in a painting, which was something the Impressionists, who squandered their energies on analysis of the motif and the breakdown of local tones, were never able to achieve.

After 1888, Cézanne's work became increasingly calm and supple, the antithesis of the dryness, savage contrasts and broken rhythms of his earlier works, which reflected the uncertainties, disappointments, anger

67   *Chestnut Trees at the Jas de Bouffan*   1885–7

68   *Harlequin*, preliminary sketch for *Mardi-Gras*   1888

69　*Mardi-Gras*　1888

70   *Portrait of Louis Guillaume*   1879–82

and difficulties of his life. Now that he had his father's fortune, he had come to terms, to a certain degree, with the lack of understanding and the irritations which he had found so hard to bear. He had no ambition left, not even that of exhibiting at the Salon. He sold some of his paintings, either directly or through Tanguy, but not out of vanity or for profit, since he let them go at absurdly low prices, ranging from forty to one hundred francs each. The eulogies which began to appear in the press certainly flattered him, but failed to dispel his sense of inferiority, while at the same time his sense of superiority enabled him to receive the harshest criticism with equanimity. He now moved less often and remained in Paris throughout 1888. When he returned to Aix, he stayed there for five years except for brief trips to Switzerland, Fontainebleau and Giverny. In short, he entered a period of tranquillity – and, having achieved complete mastery of his medium, of great productivity.

This, perhaps, is the moment to examine Cézanne's work to date. But we must avoid making hasty judgments. Cézanne himself, by his reported remarks, helped to create the false image others have perpetuated, and we must tread with care when following the path of this man who broke the laws of painting and replaced them with others which were to become a creed for painters during the next fifty years.

CHAPTER EIGHT

Painting is not the slavish copying of an object but the grasping of a harmony between several interactions . . . A powerful organizing mind is the best aid to sensation in the realization of a work of art.

CÉZANNE QUOTED BY HIS SON

The process of creation

When classical humanism was forced to give way to Christian mysticism, a new conception of form and space emerged, which was in its turn to be superseded by a revival of humanism originating in Italy. For several centuries Renaissance aesthetics were to impose on French painters a new system of optics based on perspective. This method of pictorial expression gave an illusion of reality rather than an exact transcription of it, and was more of an intellectual than a sensory process. It was subject to intangible, codified rules, that inevitably limited the artist's scope. Perspective, a convention based on ocular perception, suggested horizontal depth by means of straight lines converging towards a fixed point, but did not take into account that verticals and curved surfaces are distorted when viewed obliquely. The formulas dear to Alberti and Uccello satisfied the need felt by every artist to generalize, to create a system and to seek, from among the accidents of the universe, a solid and permanent basis for figurative art.

The Impressionists adopted Renaissance optics but abandoned the architectural stringency which had given classical painting its scenographic and mural character. Since it was no longer supported by a structural framework or underlying diagrammatic outline, the picture would have disintegrated entirely if its loss of solidary and grandeur had not, in the case of the Impressionists, been offset by the liveliness of the colour, the separation of the brush strokes and the depth of expression. It is well known how Cézanne took advantage of this. Pictorial art abandoned majestic elaboration and austerity of composition, became more pleasing and more personal, and crammed a wealth of new material into a small framework. An immediate sensation, however, cannot completely replace the intellectual power of organization and generalization; although Impressionism, by exploiting new materials for its own ends and by making light its sole concern, sharpened the painter's analytic powers, it also destroyed his desire to organize his sensations. For the first time, the painter ceased to obey a religious or moral ideal; he became conscious instead of his own unique reality. Yet he was unaware of the prison in which he confined himself, unable to perceive the narrow limits of the world he had discovered. The temple built by the architects of the Quattrocento, and reduced by the Impressionists to the size of a chapel, now needed someone capable of rebuilding it to a new plan and restoring it to its former grandeur.

Cézanne was wise enough not to adopt the methods and conventions of the Renaissance. He did not build with things which had already been used, nor did he employ the stones of a dead tradition; rather than accentuating or completing Courbet's or Daumier's realism with heavier, more sturdy forms, he began by choosing fresh materials. Once he had mastered the secrets of these new materials, he realized that he had to subordinate them to intellectual laws – a discovery which only a genius could have made, a man who, working alone, was able to rise above his age. Luckily for painting, Cézanne succeeded, at a certain moment, in exorcising the phantom of classicism which had haunted the works of his romantic youth. He ignored the appearance of reality and the direct evidence of his senses, and examined nature with the mind's eye. His undaunted perseverance was rewarded by the ability he acquired of seeing beyond the outside of things, and from then on, objects became transparent, allowing him to glimpse their inner being. He discovered in the universe the geometry that controls the whole of creation, and in his hands the Impressionist's curves become straight lines, rigid and unmoving. It is the angle that supports the form, and everything, down to a touch of colour, has volume and consistency.

He did not, however, arrive at this morphological analysis of objects, or his victory of mind over matter, by speculation or conjecture. By

71   *Still-life*   1888–90

means of sensory perception, he rediscovered one of the laws which
make up the physical world, and his humility allowed him to commune
so deeply with the inorganic world that it is a moot point whether he
invested these objects with his own human life in order to see them
subjectively, or assumed their form of existence in order to make himself
objective. When Cézanne, ignoring the natural laws of balance, made his
Blue Vase (1883–7, The Louvre) or his *Vase of Tulips* (1890–4, Art
Institute of Chicago) lean sideways, elongated the handle of his *Stone
Pitcher* (1885–7, private collection) or distended the oval of a bowl in
Still-life (1888–90, Pushkin Museum, Moscow), he did it to remind
us of the usual way in which we pick up such things, and of the everyday relationship which grows up between user and object. Vase, jug
or bowl is distorted in such a way as to suggest that the object is
stretching towards us that part of itself which our hand must grasp,

Ills. 71,
72, 74,
76

72   *The Blue Vase*   1883–7

73   *Still-life with Onions and Bottle*   1895–1900

thereby linking us to the object. Furthermore, the object is no longer a solid, indifferent block, for the power of art has animated it by releasing the everyday life concentrated in it.

Cézanne's *Still-life with Onions and Bottle* (1895, Louvre) was painted in accordance with this same sensory perspective. The base of the glass, which stands among various objects jumbled together on the table, is off-centre, and the lip has been stretched to form a semi-circle, yet the artist manages to create a balanced order out of distortion and confusion. In another picture, *Still-life with Cupid* (1895, National Museum,   *Ill. 75*

127

74   *The Stone Pitcher*   1885–7

Stockholm), the unity is achieved by a strict pyramidal composition, which elsewhere was obtained only by the skilful juxtaposition of cold and warm tones. Cézanne believed that he painted what he saw, but in fact he painted what he felt. He therefore came to invent a revolutionary new dimension which he used even for the figures he painted. Until 1888, the portraits of Mme Cézanne were usually painted in a traditional manner. After that date the angle of vision changes, and the interplay of verticals and horizontals is abandoned in favour of an unusual oblique-

Ill. 77   ness of line, which can be seen, for instance, in *Woman with Coffee Pot* (1890–4, Louvre) and even more in *Madame Cézanne in a Yellow Armchair* (1890–4, Alphonse Kahan Collection, Saint-Germain-en-Laye). Cézanne did two versions of this last portrait, which are remarkable for many reasons. In the one, in the Pellerin Collection, the model is seen full-face, and the eyes have a slight squint; a curtain and a corner of the chimney-piece, which are absent from the Lewisohn version, create depth. The

128

other portraits of Mme Cézanne painted during the same period are equally significant. The axes supporting them are broken, and the laws of stability have been violated without impairing the coherence and solidity of the painting. Although Cézanne abandoned verisimilitude, he did not move away from the truth. The lines are no longer vertical, the shapes bend, the model seems unsteady, and the arms are elongated out of all proportion and meet at the bottom of the canvas. The model is no longer placed in the enclosed space as in Renaissance paintings, but in an open space; it is less the image of a material reality than a mental picture of a spiritual reality which is more real than any other. This

75   *Still-life with Cupid*   1895

76   *Vase of Tulips*   1890–4

reality is infused with a more human quality and, through the spectator's senses, reaches the soul through the imagination.

According to reliable sources, Cézanne demanded from his models an almost inhuman degree of endurance, and only Hortense was sufficiently docile to bear with his tyranny. So terrified was he that his models might move, or that he might lose some emphasis or tone which he especially wanted to catch, that he forced them to submit to endless sittings. 'After one hundred and fifteen sittings,' Vollard recalls, 'Cézanne abandoned my portrait and left for Aix. "I am quite pleased," he told me, "with the front of the shirt." He made me leave the garment I had posed in, in his studio, so that he might on his return rework certain parts of it. "By then, I shall have made some progress. Try to understand me a little, Monsieur Vollard: the outline escapes me."'

'It is hard to imagine,' wrote Vollard, 'just how long and painful his work is some days. There were two tiny spots on the hand in my portrait, where the canvas was bare. I pointed them out to him. "If my session at the Louvre goes well this afternoon," he replied, "perhaps tomorrow I'll find the right shade to fill in those spaces. You see, if I were to put any old colour there, I should have to begin the whole painting all over again, using that as my starting point."'

The events related by Vollard took place in 1899, at a time when, one may safely assume, Cézanne was in full possession of his intellectual powers and technical abilities. They show how much persistence and concentration went into the creation of his works. This unstable, impulsive and indecisive man was a pioneer in his art. Everything was deliberately and carefully planned because he mistrusted his own impulses, although they had been an important factor in the fulfilment of his genius. With nothing to guide him but his intuition, he not only dealt the death blow to Impressionist realism but discovered a language so imaginative, so piquant, so rich in potentialities that he fully deserves the title 'the father of modern painting'.

In order to understand the novelty and originality of this undertaking, one must remember that, although he discovered the merits of geometrical simplification, he also invented a light within the painting which is

77   *Woman with Coffee Pot*   1890–4

78 *Portrait of Ambroise Vollard* 1899

subjective and haphazard, and as different from natural light as mind is from matter. 'Light,' he was later to say, 'is something that cannot be reproduced. It must be represented by something else, by colour for instance. I was pleased with myself when I discovered that.' And he had already 'discovered that' as early as 1885. From then on, he devoted the remaining years of his life to an attempt to fuse his method of construction by planes with the inherent light of the painting. He achieved this by 'creating form by means of his brush', and by using colour to mould volumes as well as to create perspective and depth. But he did not bring

79   *Boy in a Red Waistcoat*   1890–5

about this synthesis at the first attempt. First came the views of L'Estaque, painted from above, the 'cubified' houses of Gardanne, the silhouette of Mont Sainte-Victoire set against the verticals of the pine trees, the series of opulent still-lifes, the many portraits of Mme Cézanne and, immediately afterwards or perhaps concurrently, the series of the *Card Players* and the three versions of *Boy in a Red Waistcoat*.

'The culmination of art is the figure,' Cézanne once said. And the culmination of his experiments with the human figure is to be found in the *Boy in a Red Waistcoat* (Bührle Collection, Zürich), of which there

134

80 *Boy in a Red Waistcoat* 1890–5

are two other versions, one belonging to Mrs Chester Beatty (London), and the other to Paul Mellon (Washington). The three paintings date from 1890–5. In the first, which is rightly the most famous, all the component parts are arranged around the long, sturdy shape of the arm, and between the two oblique transverse lines of the table and the curtain. Depth is conveyed by the two horizontal bands of brown and yellow, and by the outlines of a picture which has been suggested in the background. The curve made by the young man's body was needed to break the rhythm of the angles on each side of the model, whereas the folded left arm restores the balance threatened by the elongation of the other arm. Cézanne painted the *Jeune homme à la tête de mort* (1894–6, Barnes Collection) in almost the same position, only the other way round. In this painting the contrast between angles and arabesques is even more marked. The triangle formed by the arm reappears in *Le Fumeur accoudé* (1890, Kunsthalle, Mannheim) and in *The Young Italian Girl* (1896, Harry Bakwin Collection, New York). It is repeated in both arms in the

Ills. 81, 82, 85–8 *Portrait of Gustave Geffroy* (1895, Pellerin Collection), and occurs in every painting of the *Card Players* series, where it is clear what constructive use the artist has made of these arms, folded at acute angles on top of the perfect horizontal of the table.

Ills. 83, 84 Cézanne had never been so concerned with reducing paintings to geometric diagrams as he was at this time: witness *The Man with a Pipe* (Courtauld Institute, London), *The Peasant* (Hahnloser Collection, Winterthur) and *The Card Players*, whether there are two card players as in the Louvre, the Courtauld Institute and the Pellerin Collection, or three as in the Barnes Collection and that of Stephen C. Clark (New York). Everywhere in these different compositions, Cézanne juxtaposed and superimposed cones and cylinders, and grouped his human figures in a pyramid shape; every straight line, curve and plane is drawn and joined together firmly. The volumes are strong and solid, and unnecessary details have been ruthlessly eliminated. Everything here is intended to emphasize the rustic simplicity of these peasants and the earthy realism of the scene. Hence the economy of movement and the extreme sobriety of the tones.

81 *Portrait of Gustave Geffroy* 1895

82   *The Young Italian Girl*   *c.* 1896

83   *Peasant*   1890–2

Cézanne began early, especially in his landscapes, to take liberties with the traditional rules of visual representation. When he painted *The Sea at L'Estaque* (1883–6), he raised the horizon, as we have seen, and lowered objects in the distance. Two or three years earlier, in *The Winding Road* (Museum of Fine Arts, Boston), he had placed the rounded shapes of the trees and the triangles of the houses one on top of the other, instead of spacing them out and creating depth in the conventional manner. As he experimented with the theme of Mont Sainte-Victoire – to which he returned no fewer than sixty times – the panorama became

84   *Man with a Pipe*   1890–4

85　*The Card Players*　1890–2

less and less complex and the melodic line more and more discreet, while
space was expressed in an increasingly intellectual manner. The truth of
this becomes apparent when one studies, in their right order, the paintings done between 1885 and 1890, all dealing with Mont Sainte-Victoire,
in particular the one in the Metropolitan Museum, New York, the
Great Pine at Mont Sainte-Victoire (Courtauld Institute, London), the *Two*
Pines at Mont Sainte-Victoire (D. Philip Collection, Washington) and the
Umbrella Pine at Mont Sainte-Victoire (Lecomte Collection). The further
Cézanne progressed in this series, the less attention he paid to the rules

Ill. 89

86   *The Card Players*   1890–2

of perspective so dear to the Italians: gradually the background becomes more important than the foreground, and the famous mountain comes nearer, grows bigger and finally covers the greater part of the canvas, while one by one the topographical features of the plain – the houses, the roads and the arches of the viaduct – disappear. Eventually, the landscape becomes simply a symphony of wild splashes of colour and moving shapes, which lead the spectator by slow stages to the heart of the geological drama, right to the undefined core, where apparent and imagined reality are one.

In her essay *Cézanne et l'expression de l'espace,* Liliane Brion-Guerry suggests that since Cézanne had set about mastering his art unaided, he was forced to retread, from its very source, the path of the painters who preceded him. She believes that the whole history of the awareness of space can be retraced in his work: that, after his 'dark period', he attempted to convey the illusion of depth by means of concentric cubes (*A Modern Olympia*) or movement suggested by curves; that, under the influence of Manet and Pissarro, he made use of light to create spatial depth; that later, in *The Winding Road,* he made use of fragmented space, lacking in unity, after the manner of Graeco-Italian mosaics; and that finally, in his desire to create a harmony similar to that of nature by projecting his mental vision on to canvas, he succeeded in unifying his compositions. All this is true to a certain extent, but it ignores the essential empiricism of Cézanne's research, a knowledge acquired by steady experimentation. It was thus that the classical concept of perspective was enriched by an element of emotion and a new spiritual dimension.

All the sacrosanct rules taught at the Beaux-Arts about the convergence of straight lines, the delimitation of the various planes and the careful grading of colour became obsolete when Cézanne set out to find for each element in the picture the place, shape and dimensions needed to express his idea. His landscapes do not suggest a motionless world, with clear-cut paths leading somewhere definite or with nature represented in mathematically tidy and rigid scenes. Rather, they show a world which moves and expands, bursting with energy, until in his last works it reaches a pitch almost of frenzy in the interplay of the shapes and colours, an interplay which depends upon a kind of geometry based upon feeling and expressed in pictorial language. In short, Cézanne neither set down nor used hard-and-fast rules for a new system of space representation. Each of his paintings was created according to the inspiration of the moment and his view of the subject. Even when objects appear dissimilar to the eye and their broken outlines and clashing colours seem to increase the confusion, they are nevertheless linked to one another by a logic of emotion which shows itself in the relations or contrasts of line and tone, in the redistribution of highlights and a careful

87   *The Card Players*   1890–2

placement of brush strokes. Cézanne was able to pierce the deceptive outer layer of things and discover within that magic world which we are incapable of seeing, a universe of potential energy, a seething mass on the brink of being, which would burst its bonds were it not for a higher will which reduces it to a homogeneous and coherent plan. It was his special gift to be able to invoke, or call forth, the essence of that which has already been created.

André Lhote, because he himself was a painter, saw this power of invocation in Cézanne particularly clearly: 'The ceaseless round of change in the visible world, where every scene obliterates itself, so to

144

88   *The Card Player*   1890–2

89   *Great Pine at Mont Sainte-Victoire*   1885–7

speak, in the course of the day, seems to achieve from time to time near perfection. It is then that one thinks of beauty, and although Cézanne was familiar with the absolute, there was no moment when such beauty could not appeal to his imagination, as it had done to Paolo Uccello and El Greco. From then on, to represent an object was, for him, simply to assert the relation it bore, at any given moment of its terrestrial evolution, to such or such a transcendental figure: a sphere, a cone or a cylinder, or any complex shape in which they were combined. And it was the emotions which helped to bring about this transformation. By comparing the object which moved him with its equivalent in a higher world, Cézanne is using a plastic metaphor and creating a new object, whose origins lie in the deepest and most mysterious recesses of human con-

146

sciousness. After Grünewald and El Greco, he is one of those rare painters of whom it can be said that he "painted with his soul". This is certainly one of the most dangerous ventures that an artist may embark on. Such an ideal implies that, in order not to be carried away into an aberrant mysticism, the artist must previously have absorbed the whole of the science of geometry by way of antidote, and that this science must form a ubiquitous and unvarying foundation to his work itself. This rule, which in a purely scientific mind would lead to aridity, draws from this sensitive nature the highest degree of expression. A large part of the emotional power of Cézanne's paintings thus stems from the fact that he *displays his methods,* instead of concealing them.'

Space in Cézanne's work excludes the notions of distance, emptiness or fullness, of metric measurement or depth. Forms which in nature are spread out horizontally are here rearranged on a single vertical plane by a mind whose concern is to gauge purely abstract dimensional relationships. This *pictorial* space is accompanied by an equally pictorial kind of light. In other words, space and light in Cézanne's work are plastic elements of his own invention. Moreover, he does not obtain this light by the simple admixture, in easily calculated proportions, of black and white or of light and dark colours, as the classical painters did, nor does he confuse it by employing the artificial light used by the Caravaggio school. He faithfully reproduces a particular colour in a particular place, but never allows it to be fragmented, as the Impressionists did, by the action of the sun's rays. 'I wanted to copy nature,' he said. 'I couldn't. But I was pleased with myself when I discovered that the sun, for example, could not be reproduced but had to be represented by something else, by colour for instance.' In fact, for Cézanne, light is born of colour, just as form is also. Colour, formerly enclosed by the outline, thanks to Cézanne's genius, now overflows it and links up with the adjacent colours, thus replacing the atmosphere of the *tenebrosi* and the luminists by another atmosphere composed of subtle interchanges, of chromatic affinities, of gradations and contrasts. No one has been able to rival Cézanne in combining chromatic values to render the quality of light and form.

Cézanne practised his technique of modelling by means of colour, of delineating form with the brush, with such freedom and authority that the Venetians themselves might have envied him. Instead of first drawing the outline of the objects on the canvas and then filling in with colour the spaces thus marked off, he drew and painted at the same time. And he painted in such a way as to bring out the structure underlying the object. He accomplished this feat by painting with thick, closely laid brush strokes, placed one against another like pieces from a mosaic. From 1888 onwards, the strokes became less clear-cut, lighter and thinner, and he never applied the last coat until the first was dry. The basic local tone is linked to intermediary tones and delicate nuances: the red of an apple, for example, turning to yellow, orange and mauve, while Mme Cézanne's face is a web of ochre, blue and pinkish and greenish grey. The *Self-portrait* in the Kunstmuseum of Bern (1879–82) and the *Self-portrait with Palette* (1885–7) reveal brutal contrasts of volume, of warm and cold colours, whereas the features of *Madame Cézanne in a Yellow Armchair* (1890–4) and of the *Boy in a Red Waistcoat* (1890–5) are reproduced with astonishing delicacy.

The older Cézanne became and the more experience he acquired, the further he allowed the melodic line to fade into the background, so preventing the internal structure from obtruding itself through the outer covering of the object; design and colour penetrate each other so that one becomes the means of identifying the other. From here on, it is easy to understand why he disliked the linearists, Raphael, Holbein, Ingres, and admired the Venetian and Spanish painters, about whom he said to Joachim Gasquet: 'They had such vitality that they were able to make the sap, their own sap, their own prodigious life, run again in all those dead trees. The flesh they painted seems like a caress and has real bodily warmth.' He might well have spoken in the same terms of his own work. Life was his one great concern. Speaking of Tintoretto, he said: 'This unhappy creature loved everything, and yet his desires were all consumed by a fire, a kind of fever, the moment they were conceived. Look at his sky! The gods turn hither and thither, there is no peace in their paradise. Their rest is a tempest. The energy which has devoured them all their lives, as it devoured him, still animates them, and after having suffered so much they now take pleasure in it. I like that.'

This criticism of another is also a confession. After such an admission, it is easier to understand the unceasing conflict between Cézanne's will and his natural impetuosity, the strictness of his moral code, his conservative opinions, and his faithful adherence to religion, morals and the established order; it is also clearer why, though he loved the people and loathed the bourgeoisie, he nevertheless behaved like a narrow-minded bourgeois. Although his early works are marked by extreme sensuality, which is all the more flamboyant because unsatisfied, he managed in maturity to overcome this. And his sensuality, once brought under control, gives body to the forms and intensifies the rhythms and colour schemes of his work. To achieve harmony and unity in his compositions, however, Cézanne, as a self-taught man, had to find a suitable means of reconciling the impulses of his emotional nature with his desire to 'establish a tradition' and to make of Impressionism 'something solid and lasting'. Hence sprang his frustrations, since the age in which he lived deprived him of the tools he needed for his task.

This is Cézanne's tragedy. Engaged on a dangerous undertaking, from which he refused to extricate himself by any virtuoso tricks, he was obliged to be content with materials which had changed very little since the time of Van Eyck, and were therefore better suited to a disciple of Ingres or Corot than to a painter who scorned all subtleties of execution, aesthetic nuances and imitative skills. Cézanne was sometimes aware of this discrepancy between his own consuming ambition and the paucity of the means at his disposal. As he was to say to Vollard, 'I have a feeling that I cannot express. What escapes me is the creation of what I feel. I shall succeed perhaps, but I am old, and it is possible that I shall die without ever having reached the ultimate achievement: to create as the Venetians created!' On the other hand, Joachim Gasquet records this very significant reaction: '"Form cannot keep pace with inspiration. Why not?" he shouted, and threw his brushes in the air and began to cry.'

The word 'realization' was often on his lips. For him, realization was a way of ensuring that objects distorted by his own sensations, and colours modified by their effect on one another, remained interdependent. It meant linking one form to another, one shade to the next, and giving stability to a form of architecture which had been deprived of its traditional means of support. But he required a method which would be at once sufficiently flexible and sufficiently strict to enable him to eliminate the discrepancies, discontinuity and diffractions of visual phenomena. He spared neither time nor effort to master this method and, when it escaped him, he rebelled with great violence. 'I cannot tear them [the objects] away,' he cried one day, 'they cling so to the point at which I am looking that it seems to me that they are going to bleed!'

His contemporaries saw only rickety tables, distorted bottles, dislocated limbs, squinting countenances and a horrifying lack of proportion. We today can discern the delicate strand of logic whereby he unites the most violent disparities. The illusions created by the juxtaposition or mere proximity of two objects are well known. As any painter will confirm, the curves of a bottle are diminished when the bottle is placed next to a round dish. Conversely, they swell out when the bottle is near a cubic box; and the more oblique the outer edge of the table, the more the bottle will seem to slant. A light surface seems larger than a dark one; consequently, the side of an object that is in the light will seem bigger if the opposite side is in the shade. That is why certain objects of Cézanne's lose their uprightness or their solidity, swell out in one part or shrink in another, and also why an apple is no longer spherical, a house no longer upright, a pine tree no longer vertical.

These permissible eccentricities have sometimes been attributed to faulty eyesight or even incapacity, but they are no more the result of ineptness than of false ingenuity. As Cézanne said to Gasquet, 'The affectation of ignorance and simplicity is the worst kind of decadence . . . Nowadays you must be able to learn for yourself. You draw in the rudiments of your profession with your mother's milk.' There was nothing wrong with Cézanne's eyes. It was his critics who were too short-sighted to see the geometry which sustains his forms, the architecture which strengthens his composition, and the modulations linking one colour with another: in short, the whole logic of his work.

CHAPTER NINE

Perhaps I was born too early. My painting
belongs to your generation rather than to mine.
I have not enough time left to express myself.
LETTER FROM CÉZANNE
TO JOACHIM GASQUET, about 1895

On the brink of fame

From the end of his romantic period on, Cézanne sought constantly for
an order that was sensitive and subjective and unlike any natural order,
for a spatial synthesis in which the vehicle and all it contained, stability
and instability, the concrete and the imaginary, became one. He finally
mastered spatial unity, which he had tried to achieve in his Auvers-sur-
Oise landscapes by Impressionist techniques, after a long and slow
struggle with construction. In 1876, while working at L'Estaque, he
wrote of the landscape before him: 'It is like a playing card. I may be
mistaken, but it seems to me to be the antithesis of the modelled form.'
Ten years later, with his houses at Gardanne, he went from this plani-
metric conception of reality to a volumetric one; and from there to a
synthetic one, as exemplified by the works done between 1888 and 1895,
in which interactions between form and colour, objects and their
surroundings, are established organically within one object, the painting
itself. From then on, reality served merely as a stimulus, whose prompt-
ings are fused with those of the imagination.

Cézanne's experience, however, was never moulded into a system,
for sometimes realism is more important than the mental image, and at
other times the reverse is true. The *Card Players* theme, which he painted
in five different versions (1890–2), is part of a stream of realism which,
starting with Le Nain, runs right through French art. The human forms
in the *Baigneurs* which was formerly in the Gourgaud Collection and is
now in the Louvre, or those in the Museum of Art in Baltimore (1892–4),
are abstract elements controlled by a skilful interplay of movement at

90 *Les Baigneurs* 1890–4

the heart of the composition. The other figures which he painted at this time are equally important. Obviously the *Harlequin* in the collection of Lord Rothschild is less realistic than, say, the portrait of *Madame Cézanne*

Ill. 91   *in the Conservatory* (Stephen C. Clark Collection), the *Man with a Pipe* (Courtauld Institute) or the *Peasant* (one in the Hahnloser Collection and one in the Pushkin Museum). Yet it is evident that we are dealing with a highly personal realism: it cannot be compared with that of a Courbet portrait or a Renoir bather, which are both imitations of tangible reality, whereas Cézanne's works are reconstructions of reality. His models have an economy of movement, a steadiness and nobility of countenance, which are never found in those of Courbet or Renoir. Courbet's *La Blonde endormie* might equally well place her arm on top of her head, instead of crossing it over her breast, and Renoir's *La Baigneuse endormie*

152

could bring hers down alongside her body without disturbing the composition. But it is impossible to imagine the *Woman with Coffee Pot* or *Madame Cézanne in a Yellow Armchair* in any other position: they form a firmly positioned whole, with their hands folded in their laps like the stoical peasants of Le Nain or the severe virgins of Russian icons. From Cézanne's lonely, rigid and unmoving figures there flows a solemn, rustic piety.

He needed twenty years of strenuous work, self-denial and sacrifice to achieve this. He had to overcome the failings of his own personality, the temptation of classicism and later those of Impressionism, but now he had finished with light vibrations and those delicate touches 'like the scales of a fish'. The strong, broad outlines and limpid style of *Dovecot* *Ills. 63,* *at Bellevue* (1888–92, Museum of Art, Cleveland) or of *Chestnut Trees at* *67* *the Jas de Bouffan* (1887) are a clear indication of what he had achieved since the Pontoise and Auvers landscapes. Another indication is the still-lifes where, in order to create mass and depth, he used contrasts between cold and warm tones carried to their highest degree of saturation; here, instead of keeping his brush strokes within the outline, he went well beyond it. The form now seems to breathe, to open itself to the pulsations of the air and touch the adjacent forms. Apples, table-cloths, plates and dishes are no longer modelled but, in Cézanne's words, 'modulated' – that is, outlined by colour rather than by black–and–white values. See, for instance, the *Vase of Flowers with Apples* (J. Laroche Collection) or the *Chest of Drawers*. Here the lesser tones are skilfully *Ill. 56* assigned to each fruit around a point of concentrated light, and the blues and greens move with great daring over the red surfaces of the apples, flowing on to the white table-cloth, where they outline the folds in the material. The same blues and greens emphasize the features of Mme Cézanne's obstinate face.

These splashes of colour interact with a subtle energy unknown before Cézanne, while the straight and oblique lines are set off one against another. All this was simply recorded by an artist who was a minute observer of the magic in familiar objects. His way of combining lines and colours, however, never repeats itself; for the imagination, if

91   *Madame Cézanne in the Conservatory* *c.* 1890

it is applied without discrimination, soon becomes stereotyped. Nothing was so uncongenial to Cézanne as adherence to a theory, formula or rule, even if such theories were the result of his own experiments. Yet every artist is permitted to discover, or rather rediscover, through a series of constantly renewed interpretations, the law that controls natural forces and human destinies. There is no limit to the patient conquest of beauty and technique when the artist feels that it will provide him with fresh sources of inspiration. By about 1890, Cézanne seemed to have said everything and yet, despite his failing health, he still had a great deal left to say.

Cézanne, at Hortense's insistence, spent that year in Paris, at 15 quai d'Anjou, one of the most beautiful quarters in the capital. However, he took no interest in the view outside his window, preferring to work in a studio which he had rented in the rue du Val-de-Grâce. At the beginning of the summer, he left for Chantilly, stayed there for five months and, when winter came, returned to the Jas de Bouffan, where Renoir came to see him. Renoir was so enchanted by Provence that he rented the house of Cézanne's brother-in-law at Montbriand for several months. A bond of sympathy, far stronger than in the past, now joined the two men. Cézanne was pleased to have a lively, intelligent and witty companion; Renoir, for his part, was far-sighted enough to see a sensitive, kindly man, a great painter who was 'passionate, single-minded, attentive and respectful of advice', beneath the rough exterior. 'How is it,' mused Renoir, 'that whenever he puts two strokes of paint on a canvas, they are always very good?'

The two friends walked together down the Tholonet road in search of a subject, and it was during this time, in 1889, that Renoir did two paintings of that theme so dear to Cézanne, the Mont Sainte-Victoire; but although they were done during the same period, they have nothing in common with Cézanne's. For Renoir the famous mountain was not the haunting, terrible mass of rock which Cézanne pushes towards us through the clear air of Provence. It is merely a hillock, and the importance given to the rounded forms of the trees in the foreground forces it back into the mists in the distance. He understood the Aix countryside no better than that of L'Estaque seven years earlier, of which he wrote to his wife, 'L'Estaque is Asnières with the sea in front of it.' Renoir recalled with his usual zest the events of his stay at Aix, Cézanne's fits of rage and despair, his outbursts whenever his 'creation' did not come fast enough for his liking, and his anger when anyone came and peered at him while he was working.

That autumn Cézanne returned to Paris and, thanks to Chocquet's intercession, was allowed to exhibit *The Suicide's House* at the Exposition Universelle of 1889. The painting, now fifteen years old, caused no scandal; worse, it was hardly noticed. In November, Octave Maus, president of the association Les Vingt in Brussels, wrote inviting him to the next exhibition organized by the group. At the same time, Maus apologized for the invitation, in view, he said, of Cézanne's contempt for shows of this kind. Cézanne immediately accepted, repudiating the 'accusation of contempt'. 'I should say,' he explained, 'that since I have had only negative results from all the studies I have executed, and since I dread criticism that cannot be answered, I had resolved to work in silence until I could produce a theoretical defence of the outcome of my efforts. But at the prospect of being in such good company, I shall not hesitate to alter my resolution.' Besides the Belgian members of the association, the 'good company' included the foreign exhibitors Sisley and Van Gogh, the latter's name appearing in the catalogue next to that of Cézanne. Flattered as Cézanne was by the invitation, he raised no objection to this juxtaposition. The exhibition opened on 18 January 1890. The public showed no interest in Cézanne's paintings; Van Gogh's aroused violent protest.

Soon the sad news of the death of Victor Chocquet reached Cézanne. He had lost a supporter and a loyal and friendly admirer, who had tirelessly devoted time and money to trying to gain him recognition. Cézanne was now at the Jas de Bouffan, where he began a series of paintings which are undoubtedly among his most successful. In 1890, in fact, he embarked on a new sequence of landscapes – ten views of the Sainte-Victoire, and started to paint his *Peasants*, his *Man with a Pipe*, his *Card Players* and several *Baigneurs*. He also began work on the *Boy in a Red*

92   *Madame Cézanne*   1890–4

Waistcoat and on his most striking portraits of Hortense: *Madame Cézanne in a Yellow Armchair, Madame Cézanne in the Conservatory* and *Woman with Coffee Pot*. Never before had he felt so close to the things and the people of his beloved Provence; never before had this son of a bourgeois father (and a bourgeois himself in so many ways) felt in such sympathy with the peasants he met on his walks in the Provençal countryside. He loved their common sense, the roughness of their personalities, their simple way of life, the serenity of their movements, and their ability to endure the long sessions he demanded of his models.

All was not well, however, at the Jas de Bouffan. Marie and her mother never stopped arguing, and only agreed in their dislike of Hortense, who, according to them, was too extravagant, lived above her means, and showed lack of feeling by living in Paris when her place was in Aix beside her husband. Cézanne begged Hortense to return to him, but she had a perfect reason for not complying: her father had just died at Lantennes in the Jura, and she had to sort out some affairs to do with his will. Since she loved travelling, she suggested to Cézanne that they should go to Switzerland afterwards; he, as usual, gave in.

They left for Besançon in June 1891, and while Hortense talked to the lawyer, Cézanne went and painted on the banks of the Oignon, a tributary of the Saône. Then they travelled to Neuchâtel. Hortense loved Switzerland, but it only bewildered Cézanne, who painted at the lake's edge with so little enthusiasm that he left many unfinished canvases behind at the hotel. He grudgingly followed Hortense to Bern, then to Fribourg, and here a strange incident occurred. By accident, Cézanne found himself in the middle of a violent anti-Catholic demonstration; profoundly affected in his beliefs and shaking with anger, he disappeared into the crowd. His wife and son waited in vain for him at the hotel until evening. For four days they looked all over Fribourg, but he was nowhere to be found. Finally, they received a letter from him, postmarked Geneva, where he had fled and where they now joined him. He offered no word of explanation for his conduct, which was caused, no doubt, as much by the journey which he had so reluctantly undertaken as by the first attacks of diabetes. Then, in penance for his disappearance or simply out of weariness, he let Hortense drag him from Lausanne to Vevey, before returning alone to Aix; for she had refused to accompany him, which further increased his mother's and sister's dislike of her.

Their bitter attacks were not altogether unfounded. Cézanne's friends, too, seem to have had little time for Hortense. They still referred to her as 'The Dumpling', a nickname she had acquired in her youth. Young Paul was no better liked. The novelist Paul Alexis called him 'The Little Dumpling'. Alexis had come to stay at Aix for a while, at the beginning of 1891. He was pleased to see Cézanne, for he was bored in that 'gloomy, desolate and enervating town'. 'Luckily,' he wrote to Zola, 'I met Cézanne again some time ago, and he has brought a little excitement into my social life; he at least feels, talks and lives. He paints every day at the Jas de Bouffan, using a labourer as a model, and one of these days I'll go and see what he's doing. Anyway, to complete the description, he believes and practises what he believes.'

Numa Coste was one of the few former pupils of the Collège Bourbon who was still friendly with Cézanne. He had given up painting to become archaeologist and historian of Aix. Since he knew that Zola was always pleased to have news of their old friend, he described Cézanne in a letter: 'I do not understand how a hard, grasping banker could have begotten someone like our poor Cézanne, whom I have seen recently. He is looking well and his health is in no danger, but he has become simple and timid and more immature than ever. He lives at the Jas de Bouffan with his mother, who, incidentally, is at odds with the Dumpling; she, in turn, does not get on with her sisters-in-law, nor do they get on with each other. Paul and his wife, therefore, go their separate ways. And it is one of the most moving things I have ever experienced to see this fine man preserve his childhood innocence, forget all the disappointments his struggles have brought him and persist, resigned yet patient, in the pursuit of a work he cannot bring to birth.'

Although there is nothing spiteful about this description, it is hardly an understanding one. To Coste, to Zola and to most of those who had known him or still knew him, and therefore should have understood him better, Cézanne was an impotent failure. His family affairs were not, however, as desperate as Coste imagined. Hortense felt like an outsider in Aix, which was a long way from the entertainments of Paris, and was bored to death. On the other hand, his mother's love and his sister Marie's energy, which relieved him of everyday worries, were essential to Cézanne, who was completely absorbed in his work. When he returned from Switzerland, the two women's complaints finally turned him against Hortense, and he threatened to halve her allowance if she refused to settle in Aix. She was therefore obliged to leave the Paris flat, and in mid-February 1892 she arrived in Aix with young Paul. Cézanne hurried them into a place he had rented for them, and returned to the Jas de Bouffan.

The arrangements at the Jas de Bouffan suited him admirably. He had a huge studio there and could use as models the gardener, Alexandre, and some of the farm labourers. They posed for *The Card Players*, for which he made several preliminary sketches. When Hortense came to the Jas, Cézanne made her sit for hours in his studio or in the conservatory while he worked at her portrait, retouching it, beginning it again or sometimes destroying it altogether. Despite his preoccupation with figure compositions he was still interested in landscapes and still-lifes. He had also discovered the endless possibilities of water-colours and used them more and more. When he was tired and felt he needed a change of air or to paint in different surroundings, he would spend a few days in or near Paris. He went to Fontainebleau in 1892, and to Monet's house at Giverny in 1894. Yet, apart from a few brief trips, he had decided to settle in the Midi, which provided the best working conditions for him. Moreover, he was afraid of falling ill and now only travelled with care. He sometimes thought of death, and prepared himself for it by praying regularly. 'I don't want to roast *in aeternum*', he confessed with disarming simplicity. Marie encouraged his religious tendencies. 'I am not experienced in life,' he confided to Ambroise Vollard, 'I lean on my sister, who leans on her confessor, a Jesuit (such people are very strong), who leans on Rome.'

Although he was only fifty-three, he already looked like an old man. But he was lively and young at heart, and Jean Royère, who met him in

93   *Self-portrait*   1890–4

94 *Cézanne in a Soft Hat* 1890–4

1896, describes him as 'large for a Provençal, rather florid, with unusually piercing eyes, an almost white beard, sparse hair, an extremely mobile face, and a rough, almost rustic appearance. He was so nervous he could not keep still. He would burst out laughing and then suddenly fall silent, and his nervous twitching showed how sensitive he was. One felt at once that he was somebody. When I said how impressed I was by one of his paintings, I saw that he grew solemn and almost trembled. He took my hand and said, "I'm a simple man. You need not pay me compliments, or lie out of politeness." "I'm telling you the truth," I replied, "and too bad if I'm wrong." Cézanne, now convinced of my sincerity, began to cry.'

There is a similar description by Edmond Jaloux: 'Suddenly, the door opened. Someone came in almost too quietly. He looked like a petit-bourgeois or a well-to-do farmer, cunning but at the same time formal. He stooped a little, his skin was tanned in reddish patches, and his forehead was bare save for some long strands of white hair. He had small, piercing, searching eyes, a slightly red Bourbon nose, a small, drooping moustache and a military goatee. That is how I saw Cézanne at our first meeting, and forever after. I listened to that slow, nasal voice of his, which had something precise and caressing about it, and I heard him talk serenely, subtly and deeply about art and nature.'

The two self-portraits which he did between 1890 and 1894 match these descriptions perfectly. In the one, *Cézanne sur fond bleu* (Pellerin Collection), he is bare-headed, while the other, in the Ishibashi Collection, Tokyo, shows him wearing a soft hat. The second of these two paintings is definitely better than the first, which was probably painted in a moment of depression.

His failing health, the complaints of Hortense, who wanted to return to Paris, the quarrels of his mother and sister with his brother-in-law Maxime Conil, all made Cézanne increasingly irritable. His trips to Paris, therefore, though brief, relieved him even if they did not comfort him. But there was nothing for him in Paris: he knew he was unwanted, and he had given up any attempt to exhibit at the Salon; he had grown more and more timid and suspicious, and avoided meeting his old friends, whom he no longer respected in any case. He sometimes went to the Louvre, or visited Tanguy, who supplied him with materials and to whom he still sent paintings, which this generous man showed to clients, telling them in a voice full of conviction: 'Here are the master-pieces of Monsieur Cézanne, a very great painter!' Tanguy, alas, died in February 1894. Five months later his collection was sold by public auction. It included six paintings by Cézanne, which went for a total of 902 francs (2,300 francs in our money); all but one were bought by the young dealer Ambroise Vollard.

The three Cézannes in the Théodore Duret sale of March 1894 had had better luck: they found buyers for 650, 660 and 800 francs respec-tively. Gustave Geffroy, writing about the sale in *Le Journal*, was full of praise for the painter: 'Paul Cézanne deserves to receive the recognition which is his by right. He is a man who looks around, is thrilled by what he sees, and wants to express his feeling of excitement in the limited space of a painting. He sets to work to find a way of doing this as truth-fully as possible.'

Geffroy did not know Cézanne personally. However, he was to be introduced to him quite soon, on 28 November, by Monet, at Giverny. Cézanne suggested, as proof of his gratitude, that he should paint Geffroy's portrait. Geffroy lived in a small flat at Belleville; Cézanne went there during April and June 1895 to work on the portrait, but never succeeded in finishing it. 'He only sketched my face,' said Geffroy, 'and he was always saying, "I'll leave that to the end," but, alas, there never was an end. One day Cézanne wrote to me, asking for the return of his easel, paints and brushes, claiming that the work was beyond him. He should never have begun, he said, and would I forgive him for giving up? I insisted on his coming back, and told him that I thought he had begun a very fine work and ought to finish it. He returned, and for about a week he appeared to be engaged in piling up thin layers of colour, as only he knew how to do, while at the same time preserving the freshness of the painting. But his inspiration had left him. He left for Aix, and a year later, on 3 April 1896, again asked for his equipment. He never returned, abandoning the painting as he had abandoned so many others.'

Geffroy was not exaggerating, and his report is confirmed by Vollard. Cézanne, paradoxically, had never been in such complete control of his powers, but he was so obsessed with perfection and so untiring in his search for the absolute that he preferred to destroy or abandon his canvases when he found that they were not completely satisfactory. Geffroy's article shows us, however, that Cézanne now had friends and admirers as well as enemies. Moreover, although he had little to do with the Impressionists and was even at variance with some of them, they loyally acknowledged his talent.

It was, however, from a young artist that he received the greatest and most flattering appreciation. In May 1891, Emile Bernard, then twenty-three, wrote with precocious insight a pamphlet called *Men of Today*, devoted to Cézanne. 'In Cézanne's work,' he wrote, 'there is that strength deriving from originality and technique which is always sought for and so seldom found in the works of this generation. This reminds me of what Paul Gauguin once said to me about Cézanne, "There is nothing so like a crust as a masterpiece" – an opinion which I here find horribly true.' Also in 1891 the critic Georges Rivière had the courage to write, 'The painter of the *Baigneuses* is a giant, but since he defies all comparison, it is easier to disown him.' Georges Lecomte praised him a year later in his essay *L'Art Impressionniste* by referring to 'the whole and healthy art of this marvellous natural genius.'

Yet, despite his rising fame, few art lovers were willing to buy Cézanne's paintings. With the death of Chocquet and Tanguy, he had lost his two strongest supporters. Caillebotte died soon afterwards, leaving to the State sixty-five paintings, four of which were by Cézanne. These, thanks to Clemenceau, who took a perverse delight in outwitting the Institute, went to the Luxembourg Museum. Cézanne's purchasers were, however, mainly his fellow painters. Six pictures were bought by Gauguin, and Claude Monet bought *Village Road* in the Duret sale of March 1894. The following year, Monet bought three more paintings in Vollard's exhibition, and Degas bought two.

Although at one time Cézanne would have been moved by such tributes, he now seemed unable to see out of the prison of his solitude.

At the beginning of 1894 he had rented a room in the rue des Lions-Saint-Paul in the Bastille district, which he left each morning to go to Alfort and Samois in search of inspiration. On 23 November he received a warm invitation from Monet to stay at Giverny, and Monet sent a similar invitation to Gustave Geffroy by the same post. 'I hope that Cézanne will come here again and join our party,' he wrote, 'but he is so strange, so afraid of meeting someone new, that I am afraid he will let us down, despite his wanting to meet you. How unlucky that man has been not to find enough support in life! He is a true artist who has come to doubt too much, and he needs to be encouraged.' When Gustave Geffroy met Cézanne, who did in fact accept the invitation, he agreed with Monet. 'He seemed immediately, to all of us, to be a strange person, timid, violent and intensely emotional.'

Cézanne's behaviour at Giverny certainly bears out this description. He stayed at the village inn, so as not to inconvenience his host, and on 28 November he was introduced to Clemenceau, Gustave Geffroy, Rodin and Octave Mirbeau, at Monet's house. Cézanne went from ebullience to despair, from noisy laughter to tears. In the afternoon, when Monet was showing his guests the garden, Cézanne suddenly threw himself on his knees before Rodin, 'to thank a celebrated man for having shaken his hand'. A few days later, Monet invited Renoir, Sisley and a few others to dinner to welcome Cézanne. During the dessert, Monet assured him, on behalf of the others, of their sincere and affectionate admiration. Cézanne burst into tears and, stuttering, cried, 'You, as well, Monet! You, too, are making a fool of me!' He then got up from the table and fled. The inn-keeper told Monet that Cézanne had left, leaving his unfinished canvases behind in his room. After he had thus broken with Monet, he soon quarrelled with the Spanish painter Francisco Oller, whose over-demonstrative friendship irked him. Cézanne was so humble and suspicious that he misinterpreted the affection which the artists of his generation showed for him. 'They think I've got a secret formula, and they want to steal it from me. But I've got rid of them all, and not one of them, not one, will get hold of me!'

He was happy only in his studio at the Jas de Bouffan, in the countryside around Aix, on the road to Tholonet or on the paths near Mont-briand and Gardanne. There at least, away from the bustle of the towns and inquiring stares, he could concentrate on his work. Painting had certainly got hold of him: he left at dawn, with his materials on his back, and did not return until the evening, exhausted. When his diabetes made the walk painful, he would go by carriage, and sometimes spent the night in the Restaurant Berne in Tholonet, sleeping in the attic in order to save money.

In 1895, Ambroise Vollard decided to organize a Cézanne exhibition in the gallery which he had opened in 1893 in the rue Laffitte. Vollard was a strange person, a Creole from Réunion, who had abandoned his studies for painting. He had succeeded in acquiring a reputation as an honest dealer, for he was gifted and impartial, but in reality his taste was guided by the established painters, and his impartiality did not prevent him from seeking a profit. Underneath the good-heartedness, he was calculating, skilful and cunning. When he started as a dealer, his great names were two conventional artists, Roybet and Innocenti, but he was looking for a painter from the avant-garde, unrecognized, with no market for his work and as defenceless as possible. He chose Cézanne and wrote to him. Cézanne replied from Aix, accepting the invitation and sending him one hundred and fifty unsigned canvases in a roll, the earliest dating from 1868 and the latest from 1894. They were too many to fit into the tiny gallery, and Vollard had the original idea of leaning most of them against the walls.

Hortense and Paul, who were still in Paris, attended the opening in November, but Cézanne stayed in Aix. This important collection, which included *Leda and the Swan* and *Woman with Coffee Pot*, covered twenty-five years of work, exhilaration and torment. Established painters like Gérôme, Quost and Gabriel Ferrier made no effort to hide their indignation, but the independents were enthusiastic, and the exhibition was a revelation even to Cézanne's friends. Pissarro wrote to his son, 'The dilettantes are astounded and cannot understand a thing, but it is great painting nevertheless. It has a staggering delicacy, diversity and classicism. . . . My enthusiasm is nothing compared with Renoir's. Even

Ills. 77, 95

167

95   *Leda and the Swan*   1886–90

Degas has fallen under the spell of this sensitive savage. Monet, everyone.
We may be mistaken, but I doubt it.' Pissarro's opinion was not, of
course, shared by the public. The paintings which Vollard had put in
the window had to be removed because crowds were gathering in the
rue Laffitte. Several important collectors came, however, notably
Auguste Pellerin, a rich industrialist, who was to build up a valuable
collection of Cézannes, and Count Isaac de Camondo, adviser to ex-King
Milan of Serbia.

The reviews varied: some were laudatory, others disparaging.
Among Cézanne's supporters was Thadée Natanson, director of *La*

Revue Blanche, who said, 'He takes his place in French painting as the master of the still-life.' Gustave Geffroy was especially enthusiastic and spoke of 'this painter who has been too much forgotten' (a phrase already used by J.-K. Huysmans in 1889), and suggested that 'once the experiment has been made, and it is high time it was made, everything obscure and chimerical in Cézanne's work will disappear, leaving an austere, simple, brutal, but nevertheless delightful body of work. . . . It is genuine, powerful and simple, harsh and subtle, and it will hang in the Louvre.' M. Denoiville, however, in *Le Journal des Artistes*, denounced 'the nightmarish imagination behind these atrocious paintings, which have overstepped the limit of ordinary practical joking', and Thiebault-Sisson, critic of *Le Temps,* said that Cézanne was 'incapable of self-criticism and of taking advantage of new ideas as clever painters had done, too inadequate, in short, to complete or fully develop what he had been the first to understand.'

The exhibition was an honourable failure. Meanwhile, at Aix, Cézanne went on painting, apparently oblivious of the stir he was causing in Paris. He saw no one but Emperaire, Solari and Coste. This last wrote to Zola in April 1896: 'Cézanne is very depressed and often a prey to dark thoughts; but his self-pride is at times satisfied, and his works are having a success in the sales that is quite new to him.' Cézanne had renewed acquaintance with an old school friend, Henri Gasquet, a retired baker. One day, Gasquet introduced him to his son, Joachim, a twenty-three-year-old poet, who had just seen two of Cézanne's works in an exhibition organized by 'Les Amis des Arts', a society of amateur painters in Aix. Although Cézanne's paintings had provoked some malicious remarks, Joachim said how much he admired them. 'Cézanne blushed,' he says, 'and began to stutter; then, drawing himself up, he shot me such a terrible look that I, too, blushed, from top to toe. "Don't make fun of me, boy!" he shouted and, with a mighty blow of his fist, he made the table shake, the glasses tinkle, everything clatter. I don't think I've ever been so frightened. He seized me, saying, "Sit down." Then, to my father, "Young Henri is kind," and the angry tone in his voice melted and he became gentle. "Above all it's the *Sainte-Victoire* you've been struck by! So you like that painting? Tomorrow I will send it to you, signed."' Cézanne did, in fact, give him the landscape, which is now in the Courtauld Institute.

For a week, the poet and the painter met almost daily. Then, on 15 April 1896, Cézanne refused to see him, on the ground that he was going to Paris. But on the 30th Gasquet and his wife, Marie, ran into Cézanne in the cours Mirabeau. Cézanne pretended not to have recognized them, but that evening he wrote a letter of apology. 'You do not know what a sad state I have been brought to! I am not master of myself, that non-existent man, and must you play the philosopher and finish me off? But I curse those ———s and rascals who, for fifty francs per article, have dragged me into the public eye. If I had been allowed to fulfil

96 *Sainte-Victoire* 1896

97 *Portrait of Joachim Gasquet* *c.* 1896–7

myself, it is I who would have remained sitting in a corner with my painter friends, drinking a mug of beer. I still have a good friend from those days. He never made it, but that does not stop him from being a lot more of a painter than all those wastrels with medals and decorations. It's enough to drive you mad! And you want me, at my age, to believe in something? You are young, and I can understand your wanting to succeed, but all I can do in my position is to lie low, and if it were not for the fact that I love the sight of my country so much, I would not be here.'

The two men were reconciled the following day, and this marked the beginning of a firm friendship. Cézanne gave Marie Gasquet a painting of bathers and embarked on the portrait of Joachim which now hangs in the Gallery of Modern Art in Prague. His letter to Joachim attests to his disillusionment with human nature at this time. His unstable and suspicious nature was partly to blame, but so was his loneliness. He had broken, one by one, the bonds which tied him to the past. Having already quarrelled with Zola, he hated the idea of seeing Zola's friends, Paul Alexis and Numa Coste. Zola spent a few days in Aix with Coste, but the latter made no effort to bring about a reconciliation. Renoir's caustic wit had become unbearable to Cézanne, and he had had no contact with him since 1889. Nor had he been in touch with Monet since his outburst at Giverny. He met him for the last time, by accident, in the rue d'Amsterdam, and pretended not to have seen him. He even neglected his kind friend Pissarro because he was a Jew, a socialist and a champion of Dreyfus. Of all his old friends, Solari, the sculptor, was the only one he still liked. On top of this, his diabetes, left untreated and worsened by his mania for work, increased his unsociability. In early summer 1896, he decided to go to Vichy for a cure; this tired him out and he went to rest at Talloires on Lake Annecy. But he never rested. Each day, he sketched or worked on a painting, and at Talloires he did one of his most remarkable landscapes, *The Lake of Annecy* (Courtauld Institute). He returned to Paris during the winter and took lodgings, first in Montmartre and then, in 1897, in the rue Saint-Lazare. In 1898, he rented rooms for a while in the rue Hégésippe-Moreau and there, for the first time, he hired a woman to pose for him naked, something which he had never dared to do in Aix.

In about 1895, his contemporaries might have thought that this fifty-six-year-old artist had reached the height of his career. Besides innumerable sketches and water-colours, he had produced all his most substantial, harmonious and balanced paintings: two hundred landscapes, fifty-four still-lifes, twenty-one bathers, eighteen portraits of Hortense,

98   *The Lake of Annecy*   1896

three of his son and seven self-portraits. Yet, despite the advance of illness and old age, Cézanne was soon to find new powers within himself, as if his enormous patience and craving for solitude had accumulated in him deep reserves of energy. Tempted by a baroque restlessness and violence, his genius now sought a less stable definition of itself, something tenser and more exuberant, as in the days when he strove naïvely after romantic rhythms and effects, whose secrets were to be revealed to him only at this much later date.

CHAPTER TEN

Life is appalling!
CÉZANNE

Old age and rejuvenation

Towards 1895 Cézanne entered the period which some of his biographers call 'baroque old age' and others 'the culmination'. If, for
instance, one compares *Rocks at L'Estaque* (1882–5), *The Great Pine at
Sainte-Victoire* (1885–7, National Gallery) and *Dovecot at Bellevue*
(1888–92, Museum of Art, Cleveland) – serene and carefully constructed
pictures whose feeling for architectural balance leaves no room for
fantasy – with landscapes painted at the end of Cézanne's life, one sees
that instead of progressing towards an increasingly rigid structural order,
he found himself faced with new demands on his sensitivity. He felt that
by breaking the laws of reality he was in danger of destroying it, and
that he needed a more personal contact with nature. 'I must get close to
reality,' he said to Gasquet. 'I want it whole. Otherwise I would be doing,
in my own way, what I most dislike in the Beaux-Arts: I would be
getting a preconceived idea in my head and modelling the truth on it;
whereas what I really want is to model myself on the truth.'

His latent lyricism and long-suppressed sensuality were trying to
break out, and they brought about a change, if not a regression, in his
vision of things and in his technique. He still painted landscapes with the
same affection, but he now gave himself over to the rapture of pure
sensation. Mont Sainte-Victoire, in particular, had always inspired him,
and he painted it no fewer than eleven times between 1895 and 1906.
Bernard Dorival has rightly remarked that Cézanne 'Provençalized' all
the other views which he painted, particularly those done on the Ile-de-
France and in Savoy. *Rocks at Fontainebleau* (1894–8, Metropolitan

175

99 *Rocks in a Wood* 1894–8

Ills. 98,
100, 101 Museum of Art, New York), *Rocks and Trees at Bibémus* (1900–4, Musée
du Petit Palais, Paris) and *The Lake of Annecy* (1896, Courtauld Institute, London) are all treated in the same manner. In fact, it was
less Provence than himself that Cézanne found everywhere and at all
times, more his own nature, which now was no longer restrained, than
external nature. He had been trying, with varying success, to reach a
synthesized perception of reality and a homogeneity of spatial construction by the exercise of his intelligence and will. This unified vision and

inner consistency of execution he now achieved by allowing freer rein to his impulses.

Had he, then, reverted to the romanticism of his youth? It is legitimate to link his earliest and his latest works, so long as only a general correspondence is understood. In his early works his emotional personality was too much in evidence, but in the later ones his lyricism obeyed a hidden order which was the outcome of a lifetime of work and an ever narrowing and more subtle communion with things. This man who claimed that he wanted to reach down to the 'geological foundations of

100   *Rocks at Fontainebleau*   1894–8

101　*Rocks and Trees at Bibémus*　1900–4

the landscape', and 'to marry the brows of hills with a woman's curves', stubbornly sought to uncover the hidden relationships between earth's various beings. In one of his still-lifes the folds in the table cloth are like the peaks of the Mont Sainte-Victoire; the rocks of Bibémus are painted with the same strokes as those used to 'modulate' the rough faces of the peasants; the bodies of his bathers have something in common with the trees framing them and the clouds above them. The plastic elements which he introduced merge at once with the composition and the universal order of things.

102 *Seated Man* *c. 1898–1900*

103   *Still-life with Curtain*   1895–1900

By looking at some of the works that he did around 1895 or 1896 – the *Baigneuses* in the Museum of Art, Baltimore, the *Great Pine* in the São Paulo Museum, the *Still-life with Cupid* in the National Museum, Stockholm, the *Portrait of Joachim Gasquet* and the *Seated Man* in the National Gallery, Oslo – we can see that Cézanne's lyricism seems to have freed itself from his former way of working. The geometry of the work often vanishes behind the stress now laid on form and colour, which, over the years, became almost frenetic. Never before had Cézanne come so close to the mystery of nature, and never had the contemplation of the external mattered so little to him. The object disembodied itself and became a moving part of space and light, and his brush acquired an

Ill. 102

alacrity which gave the painting the liveliness of a sketch and the appearance of improvisation. His art had reached the stage at which, all science having been transcended and everything gained by experience having been absorbed, feeling became the ultimate law governing any new experience or new science. 'I want knowledge,' he said, 'in order to achieve deeper feeling, and I want feeling in order to achieve deeper knowledge. I want to be a real classic, to become classical through nature

104   *Still-life with Fruit*   1890–4

105   *Still-life with Skull and Candlestick   c.* 1900

and feeling.' But he believed that the feeling which brought about the fullness and arrangement of the volume now ensured, by the vitality of form and colour, the unity of space and light. Nature, which Cézanne wanted to observe faithfully, hardly ever comes into his world. Free at last from aesthetic and technical worries, he was carried forward by an unpredictable fever, and began to use an increasingly free language, built on more sensitive material than previously, imbued with a disturbing light and more dramatic shadows.

This rejuvenation was promoted by a series of unhappy circumstances in Cézanne's life: the advance of his illness, his extreme loneliness, the death of his mother on 15 October 1897 and his preoccupation with death (expressed in the frequent appearance of skulls in his works). Cézanne's suffering and misfortune might well have destroyed his last powers and his will to work. Instead, his creative activity increased, and he was inspired by that renewal of energy which is to be found in the old age of many great artists. Moreover, now that his worth was finally being recognized, his self-respect was at least partly satisfied.

In 1895 he was overjoyed to hear that three of his paintings were going to hang in the Musée du Luxembourg. In 1899, 1901 and 1902 he exhibited at the Salon des Indépendants, where the artistic élite gave him an enthusiastic reception. In 1900 Maurice Denis painted his famous *Homage to Cézanne*, which showed Bonnard, Roussel, Vuillard, Redon, *Ill. 106* Sérusier, Mellerio, Ransan, Vollard, Denis and his wife gathered round one of Cézanne's still-lifes; it was exhibited at the Salon in 1901. Three of Cézanne's paintings were shown in 1900 at the centenary of the Exposition Universelle. His fame now reached abroad: an Italian collector, Egisto P. Fabbri, bought sixteen of his paintings; in 1900 one of his landscapes was purchased by the National Gallery of Berlin, and in 1901 he agreed to send several paintings to an exhibition entitled 'La Libre Esthétique' in Brussels.

It was not long, however, before his suspicious nature took offence at these tributes. 'What does this prove?' he said. 'They're getting ready to play a trick on me.' When the Berlin National Gallery purchased one of his works, he remarked, revealingly: 'They won't have me at the

106　Denis *Homage to Cézanne*, detail　1900

Salon for all that!' He was, in fact, naïvely waiting for official recognition, which never came. The 'messieurs de l'Institut' remained adamant, and it seemed unlikely that he would ever be awarded the Légion d'Honneur which he coveted. In 1902, Octave Mirbeau approached M. Roujon, director of the Beaux-arts, but was rebuffed. 'I will give an award to anyone you like,' he was told, 'Monet, Sisley, Pissarro, but not Cézanne. You see, I have to comply with public taste, not anticipate it.' Two years later Roger Marx tried to obtain an award for Cézanne from the Ministry of Commerce in connection with the Exhibition of Saint-Louis. But Cézanne's work was turned down by the jury, and the attempt failed.

Cézanne had only himself to blame for his isolation. For instance, in Paris he would meet such friends as Guillaumin and Signac in the street and refuse to speak to them. He was pleased to see Solari and Joachim Gasquet at Aix, and began to paint portraits of Joachim, his wife and his father, but never finished them. He made new friends, the painters Emile Bernard and Charles Camoin and the writers Edmond Jaloux, Joseph d'Arbaud, Xavier de Magallon and Léo Larguier. What most attracted him in these young men was a liveliness of feeling so like that which he

still possessed, despite his age. But if he suspected insincerity or calculation on their part, he would break with them immediately. In this way
he was estranged from Gasquet, whose eloquence hid a cunning which
ended by antagonizing Cézanne. At the risk of regretting it later, he often
allowed his instinctive mistrust to disappear when he was moved by
words of sympathy; he then became friendly and talkative. Everyone
who knew him was agreed on this point. 'Paul was not a savage, just a
recluse,' his brother-in-law Maxime Conil was to say. Under his rough

107   *Forest Landscape*   1892–4

exterior, he was a child at heart, which explains his alternating moods of exuberance and despair. He could be moved by a trifle. Solari's son recalls the trip which he took with his father and Cézanne to Mont Sainte-Victoire, where the old painter seemed as carefree as a truant schoolboy. Joachim Gasquet describes one of their walks, in April 1896, when Cézanne, enthusing over the rebirth of nature, had cried out with childish delight: 'This is the first time I've seen the spring!' Edmond Jaloux was lunching with the Gasquets when Cézanne entered un-

108   *Pine-tree near Aix*   1885–7

announced and sat down at the table. At that moment a ray of light fell on a plate of peaches and apricots. 'Look!' he cried, with a gesture of delight, 'how tenderly the sun loves those apricots! It envelops them all, illuminating them from all sides. But see how mean it is with the peaches and how it only lights up one side of them!'

In the autumn of 1896 the Cézannes returned to Paris and rented a flat in Montmartre, where Cézanne painted *The Young Italian Girl* (Harry Bakwin Collection, New York). The family moved in December to the rue Saint-Lazare, where Cézanne fell ill with influenza and remained in his room until the end of January 1897. When the fine weather came, he left for Fontainebleau and made many studies of the trees and rocks in the forest. He then went to Mennecy, near Corbeil, staying at an inn called the 'Belle Etoile'. At the end of May he returned to Aix to discover that his mother's health had seriously deteriorated. He decided to stay at the Jas de Bouffan to look after her. But his sister Marie, not wanting such a burdensome nurse, managed to dissuade him, probably without much difficulty, since his work was his main concern. His mother died on 15 October. 'He was not present on the day of the funeral,' wrote Emile Bernard, 'because he had to work, although no one perhaps had loved her or wept for her as he had.' He was overwhelmed by the loss, and sought in painting the relief which no human being could provide.

Mont Sainte-Victoire had now become such an obsession with him that he went to Bellevue, Bibémus and the Barrage Zola in order to stare at it with renewed wonder each day. He painted it again and again, with increasingly dramatic effects: the sacred mountain rises out of a landscape tormented by an inner fire which makes the earth tremble and the air vibrate. The paintings of the mountain in the collection of Cézanne's son (1897), in the Robert H. Tannahill Collection, Detroit (1897), and in the Pushkin Museum (1898) all suggest the mood, although the violence is tempered by a rigid arrangement of the irregularities of the plain and the atmospheric elements. Cézanne often walked, either alone or with Emperaire or Solari, to the Bibémus quarry, where he had a small cottage. Here he could leave his materials and eat his meal of bread, cheese and nuts; for although he was rich, he still lived modestly and ate simply. But whenever Solari's presence gave him the excuse, he was only too delighted to eat one of those copious meals which Mme Berne produced from the Tholonet kitchen.

Solari's son Emile has left us this vivid description of Bibémus: 'Old stone quarries have left strange caves there. After crossing a large expanse of ground planted with small trees, you come upon an unforgettable landscape, with Mont Sainte-Victoire in the background, and to your right the successive outlines of Montaiguet and

109   *The Millstone*   1898–1900

110 *Mont Sainte-Victoire Seen from Bibémus* 1898–1900

the hills of Marseilles. It is at the same time vast and intimate.' Cézanne
gave a feeling of intense heat and an apocalyptic sense of upheaval
to the green undergrowth and yellow-orange rocks of Bibémus.
This is especially noticeable in three paintings done in 1898, *Rocks at*
Bibémus (Folkwang Museum, Essen), *The Millstone* (C. S. Tyson Collection) and *Mont Sainte-Victoire Seen from Bibémus* (Museum of Art,
Baltimore), as well as in *The House with Cracked Walls* (formerly in
the Matsukata Collection, Tokyo), a masterpiece in which a hovel
surrounded by rocks and trees displays its wounds, much as the faces

Ills. 109,
110, 111

189

of peasants show theirs. His sense of pathos never reacted so strongly as it did to the masses of tangled vegetation, furrowed earth and caved-in stones of Bibémus and the Château Noir. This chaos offered a formidable challenge to an artist so deeply concerned with order and clarity. The wild scenery of Provence, more than the forests of Chantilly and Fontainebleau, stimulated his greatest talents, precisely because he found it so hard to express. He spent hours in the depths of the woods, studying the mass of rocks and the dense trees which were so well suited both to his aims as a painter and to his taste for solitude. Of the drawings and water-colours he did at this time, there is no exact record. As for the paintings, one should mention in particular *The Red Rock* (Walter Collection, Paris), *View of the Château Noir* (Reinhart Collection, Winterthur) and the version in Sir Kenneth Clark's collection at Salwood Castle, *In the Park of the Château Noir* (Soubies Collection, Paris) and *Forest Landscape* (Kunsthaus, Zürich), all of which date from 1896–9.

After the death of her mother, Marie Cézanne decided to live in Aix, where she was within easy reach of a church and could do charity work. Hortense and her son were more determined than ever not to leave Paris; so Cézanne, who was incapable of living alone or of managing his property, sold the Jas de Bouffan. It was bought by a M. Granet in 1899. In October 1898 Cézanne left for Paris and went to live with his family at 15 rue Hégésippe-Moreau. Ambroise Vollard, who had just arranged a new exhibition of Cézanne's works, asked him to paint his portrait (Petit Palais, Paris). Cézanne worked on it for a good three months with his usual care, and Vollard calmly submitted to his demands. He tells some amusing stories about these sittings. He went to Cézanne's studio every morning, and in the afternoon Cézanne worked on the *Baigneuses* or went to the Louvre to draw. If he was dissatisfied with the studies he had made at the museum the day before, or if he was disturbed by the slightest sound, he would lose his temper, put down his brushes and declare that he could work only in peace and quiet. Vollard was both amused and worried, for he could never be certain that Cézanne would not rip up the canvas in a fit of anger.

111　*The House with Cracked Walls*　*c.* 1896

112   *Mont Sainte-Victoire and the Château Noir*   1898–1900

He concealed his weariness and avoided subjects of conversation that might annoy Cézanne, such as comments on art or literature, or on the Dreyfus case, which was then shocking public opinion. Finally, after one hundred and fifteen sittings, Cézanne abandoned the portrait, promising to take it up again some day. 'By then, I shall have made some progress,' he said. 'Please try to understand – the outline escapes me.'

During the summer of 1899, he returned to the Pontoise area, which held memories for him of twenty years earlier. He rented a room at

Montgeroult. Here Louis Le Bail, a painter who lived in Marines and a great admirer of Cézanne's, came to see him. Cézanne received him warmly, as he always did in such cases, for he was unsociable only when he thought that people were trying to exploit him, or simply when they failed to live up to his expectations. Although he distrusted the intellectuals and painters of his own generation, he always showed friendliness to young artists. 'I think the younger painters much more intelligent than the others,' he wrote to his son; 'the old ones see in me only a dangerous rival.' He despised the nouveaux

113   *Le Château Noir*   1904–6

riches, but loved the lower classes, the workers and peasants. 'They all remembered him with loving affection,' wrote Gasquet; 'he was immensely generous to them, not only with his money but with his heart and mind.' His consideration for his coachman, for instance, who drove him to the places where he painted, was touching. Gasquet tells the following story: 'The sun was beating down; we were half-way up a steep slope and the horse and driver, exhausted, had fallen asleep. Cézanne sat in the full sun, without a word, without moving, so as not to disturb them, and waited for them to wake up, innocently rubbing his eyes so that it should appear that it was he who had fallen asleep.' Also according to Gasquet, 'On the hilly roads of Eguilles, his instinct was always to help others, to push a peasant's overloaded cart or take a pitcher of water from some old woman's frail hands.'

On several occasions Cézanne went out painting with Louis Le Bail, with whom he felt at ease and could talk freely. Then suddenly, over some trivial incident, he broke with him and wrote him this note: 'Monsieur, The somewhat cavalier manner with which you allow yourself to come to my house is not to my liking. In future, be so kind as to announce your visit. Also, please give the glass and canvas which I left in your studio to the person I am sending you. Yours truly.'

Cézanne was now at Aix. The Jas de Bouffan had been sold, and his sisters had even gone so far as to burn their parents' furniture and possessions, which made Cézanne extremely unhappy. One evening he arrived at Gasquet's house, looking upset. 'They have even burnt the armchair in which Papa used to take his siesta,' he said, 'and the table where he worked on his accounts. He always used that one, ever since he was a boy.' The armchair was the one in which his father and Emperaire had posed for him. In fact, the 'relics' whose loss Cézanne so mourned were useless objects which only gathered dust and had no sale value. Louis-Auguste would not have dreamt of keeping them, much less of repairing them. In his state of confusion, Cézanne allowed Marie to organize his life. She had rented a small flat for him in a private house at 23 rue Boulegon and had had the attic fitted up as a studio. Knowing that her brother was incapable of looking after himself, she

114 *Mountain Stream* 1882–5

engaged a housekeeper, Mme Brémond. The rue Boulegon was quite near the cathedral of Saint-Sauveur, which enabled him to go to early mass each morning. Marie had provided for everything.

Cézanne was no longer in touch with Monet, Renoir or Pissarro, who were now successful, even fashionable, painters. There were signs that he himself was beginning to be appreciated. When Mme Chocquet died in 1899, her husband's collection was sold by auction in July of the same year, and thirty-two Cézannes went for a total of 50,000 francs (about 350,000 francs in our money). *The Forest Road* was sold for 1,200 francs, and *The Little Bridge* for 2,000. Durand-Ruel paid 1,500 francs for *Mountain Stream,* and some 4,400 for *Mardi-Gras,* which he later resold to the Russian collector Shchukin. Thadée Natanson bought *La Côte du Galet à Pontoise* for 2,600 francs and resold it in 1908 for 6,600. *The Suicide's House*, which is now in the Louvre, fetched the highest price, being purchased by Camondo for 6,200 francs. *Farm in Normandy* went for 1,400 francs and was resold for 14,200 in 1907. That same year, at the Count Doria sale, *Melting Snow,* a picture which Cézanne painted in 1879 from a photograph of the Rouart family's estate at Melun, was bought for 6,750 francs. The purchaser was Claude Monet.

Thus, in the five years since the Tanguy sale, the average price of a picture by Cézanne had increased tenfold. It was still, however, far below that commanded by the Impressionists. At the Chocquet sale of 1899, Manet's *Road Menders in the Rue de Berne* sold for 13,500 francs, Monet's *View of Argenteuil* for 11,500 francs and Renoir's *La Grenouillère* for 20,000 francs (140,000 in our money). Cézanne did not seem to be surprised, or even pleased, by the high prices his paintings were now fetching. After all, it merely confirmed what he had told his mother in 1874: 'Now is a bad time to sell, for the bourgeois are loath to part with their pennies; but that will come to an end.' Nor did he appear to envy the Impressionists their sudden good fortune. He was obsessed by the need to 'create', and he strove so passionately for the goal he had set himself that he hardly gave thought to material gains, to fame, comfort or money; as for decorations, his only ambition

115 *Farm in Normandy: The Orchard* 1885–6

was, childishly, to receive the Légion d'Honneur. All this goes to prove his humility and self-effacement. Despite the considerable inheritance from his father, he went on living as though he were poor, renting modest flats, eating simply and dressing shabbily. In his youth, he had often spent the night on a bench in the waste land round the Jardin du Luxembourg, placing his shoes under his head as a pillow for fear that a tramp might steal them while he slept. Now in his old age and with a large income, he was not averse to sleeping in the attic of the restaurant Berne and sometimes even in a barn.

116 *Self-portrait with Béret* 1898–1900

He was unconcerned about the fate of his works, carried them with him from place to place and left them behind in lodgings, hotel rooms or even on the sites where he was working. He gave them away to anyone lucky enough to have pleased him or have done him some service; to Monet, Renoir, Pissarro, Gustave Geffroy and the Gasquets. He even offered one to the coachman who drove him each day to Tholonet. 'Well, he was pleased and thanked me for it,' he told Joachim Gasquet, and added gently, 'but he left it with me; he forgot to take it.' Vollard recalls how he went to Aix one day to look for paintings by Cézanne and unearthed some with people who took no care of them and were delighted to part with them for a few hundred francs. Having collected several canvases from one such house, he was leaving when a voice called from a window: 'Eh, Artist, you've forgotten one!' – and a Cézanne landscape crashed on to the pavement at his feet.

Cézanne knew that he was the greatest painter of his age. He was also far-sighted enough to judge the distance he had yet to cover: 'I am too old,' he confessed to Emile Bernard in 1904; 'I have not fulfilled myself, nor will I ever fulfil myself.' But at the same time he was quick to add, with pride: 'I am the first to tread the road that I have discovered.' Also in 1904, he is reported as saying, 'You well know that there's only one painter in the world, and that's me!' Jean de Beucken, in a monograph on Cézanne, claims that the painter identified himself with Frenhofer, the hero of Balzac's *Le Chef-d'oeuvre inconnu*. Frenhofer scorns the works of his youth and speaks of nothing but the picture he has been working on for years; but he will let no one see it. He finally shows it, however, to Porbus and the young Poussin, who are amazed to find, contrary to their expectations, a chaos of lines and colours, out of which emerges, in defiance of all logic, a beautifully drawn foot. They are even more surprised to hear the old painter refer to this formless work as the masterpiece he believes it to be. 'This tale, written in 1839,' writes Jean de Beucken, 'was not generally understood until a century later; Cézanne had come to grasp its full meaning in about 1900, ahead of his time. . . . He had read and re-read it, and he was not joking when he cried out one day, "I am Frenhofer!"'

Cézanne's rising fame, the high prices his works now fetched at public auctions and the respect shown him by the local intelligentsia, far from disarming his critics in Aix, only increased their antagonism. In their eyes, he was a maniac, a lunatic, a simpleton, and the reputation he enjoyed in Paris was due, in their opinion, to his cunning and deceit. This aging artist, dressed in threadbare clothes, daubing away at canvases which anyone could produce, provided the petty and prejudiced townsfolk with ample gossip. He was a constant target for misunderstanding and malice; they even mocked him to his face. Once when he was about to set up his easel on some private property, he was chased away. Henri-Modeste Pontier, who had succeeded Honoré Gibert as principal of the art school and director of the museum, swore that never, so long as he lived, would a painting by Cézanne hang in the local museum; and he managed to keep his word. Moreover, even today there is not one work by Cézanne in his own home town. His fellow townsmen have apparently not forgiven him for his excellence, which they regarded as an insult.

This hostility forced him further into isolation. He dared not even walk down the Cours Mirabeau, and whenever he went to his studio in Les Lauves, street urchins ran after him, throwing stones. His diabetes prevented him from walking straight and they took him for a drunkard. His extreme sensitivity magnified such humiliations. Apart from the loss of all his old friends – Emperaire, Marion, Valabrègue, Paul Alexis and Sisley – Zola's death, on 29 September 1902, upset him deeply despite their quarrel. He was at home when the gardener abruptly told him the sad news. Cézanne turned white, his eyes filled with tears and, waving his arms about, he shouted at the man, 'Go away, go away!' He refused to move from his studio for the rest of the day. In the evening, he went to see Solari, the only person who would understand his grief.

These blows intensified his instability and disillusionment with human nature. He avoided the people of Aix, and was suspicious of old friends, except for Solari; but he eagerly welcomed all young people, provided they were newcomers. In 1901, he was introduced

117　*Man with a Pipe*　c. 1895–1900

to Léo Larguier, a twenty-year-old poet who came from a farming family in the Cévennes, and to Charles Camoin, a painter from Marseilles, who were both doing their military service in Aix. Larguier introduced him to a friend of his, Louis Aurenche, a civil servant posted in Aix. Cézanne took an immediate liking to the young men and was delighted to welcome them to his house. Knowing that they were hard up, he often invited them to a meal. Moreover, since they took no interest in painting, the conversation could run smoothly, without touching on this sensitive subject. In the autumn, Larguier was demobilized, and his parents invited Cézanne to spend a few days on their farm. He went, accompanied by his wife and son, and his good humour won him the liking of everyone. He took every opportunity to relax or, as he put it, to 'uncork' himself. This account helps one to understand his affection for Solari, who was earning a meagre living in Aix by his sculpture: Solari was a cheerful companion and provided Cézanne with a means of relaxation. One night, Vollard recalls, Cézanne's neighbours in the rue Boulegon heard cries and shouts coming from his flat; thinking that someone was being murdered, they rushed in to wake up Mme Brémond. 'Don't worry,' she said. 'M. Cézanne and M. Solari are discussing painting.'

He also indulged in other eccentricities, which were gloated over in Aix, to the displeasure of his sister Marie. She urged Mme Brémond to watch him more closely. Since he was very generous with his money to the poor, especially the beggars who stood on the steps of the cathedral, she feared that he would squander his fortune and instructed Mme Brémond not to allow him out in future with more than fifty centimes in his pocket. It was also on her insistence that Mme Brémond burned the sketches for the *Baigneuses*, on the grounds that they were obscene and a disgrace to the family name.

In March 1903, Zola's widow put up for auction most of her husband's collection. There were ten paintings by Cézanne, dating back to his youth: *The Rape* went for 4,200 francs (29,000 francs in our money), and Auguste Pellerin bought a portrait for 950 francs and two still-lifes for 3,000 and 900 francs respectively. These were reasonably high prices.

A Monet landscape in the same sale fetched only 2,805 francs (18,700 francs today), and two Pissarros went for a mere 920 and 500 francs. This sale provided Cézanne's opponents with a fresh opportunity for venting their anger. Henri Rochefort, a polemical and mediocre art critic, wrote in *L'Intransigeant* on 9 March:

'There were in the sale a dozen works, landscapes and portraits, by an ultra-Impressionist called Cézanne. Particularly grotesque was the head of a dark-haired man with a beard, whose cheeks, slapped on with a trowel, looked as if they fallen prey to eczema. [He was doubtless referring to the *Head of an Old Man*, now in the Louvre.] The other *Ill. 118* works by this artist all seemed to be openly sneering at Corot, Théodore Rousseau, Hobbema and Ruysdael. If M. Cézanne had been in the cradle when he made these daubings, we should have nothing to say. But what are we to think of the head of a school who claimed to be lord of Médan and yet helps to spread such artistic lunacy?'

According to John Rewald, this article caused an enormous stir, especially in Aix, where people had thought that the Parisians only *pretended* to admire Cézanne's work in order to make fools of them. When they read Rochefort's review, they made no effort to conceal their delight that there was still someone in Paris who spoke truthfully. Three hundred copies of *L'Intransigeant*, says Gasquet, were slipped 'under the door of everyone, far and wide, who might have shown some sympathy for Cézanne.' Every morning Cézanne himself received a copy, along with a serious of anonymous letters demanding that he 'remove himself from the town he had shamed'. However hurt he may have been by this outburst of hatred, he made no complaint but simply went on painting, refusing to let anyone or anything distract him from his work. 'The kind of work which succeeds in making some progress in its own field,' he wrote in a letter to Emile Bernard, 'is sufficiently rewarding in itself to compensate for the misunderstanding of fools.'

Nevertheless, life was not easy. When it rained or when the mistral was strong, he found the trip to Tholonet most uncomfortable, particularly in his delicate state of health. He loved to contemplate this

118   *Head of an Old Man*   1860–5

spot, a place he had discovered to the north of Aix, and to work there in the blinding sun to the chirp of the crickets. In bad weather, he had to stay in his studio in the rue Boulegon, where he lacked both light and space. He thought of building a studio to his own requirements, in as quiet a place as possible, pleasant and yet close to the town. One day he saw, on the chemin des Lauves, an old olive tree which seemed to have been waiting for him there for years. He was moved. 'He touched it,' says Gasquet, 'spoke to it and sometimes when he left in the evenings, even hugged it.' This was in 1901. Cézanne bought the land, built the studio he wanted, spacious enough to permit him to undertake large works. He finished *Les Grandes Baigneuses* there, which he had begun in 1898.

Mme Cézanne and her son, now aged thirty, came to spend the winter of 1901–2 in Aix. According to Léo Larguier, who was invited to dinner with them, Cézanne was barely civil to his wife but seemed to adore Paul. He constantly praised his physical strength and business sense, the qualities, in fact, which he himself lacked. This business sense of Paul's was extremely annoying to Vollard, since the young man would, for a commission, send his father's paintings to other dealers, notably to the Bernheims. Larguier left Aix, as did Camoin and then Aurenche, and Cézanne was left alone. He had almost stopped seeing the Gasquets, whom he had come to suspect of trying to 'get hold of him', of having joined forces with 'the intellectual clan'. He desperately needed the company of the young, but he had to wait until 1904 to find someone he liked. In February of that year, Emile Bernard paid him a first visit. He had already expressed his admiration for Cézanne some fifteen years earlier, although he then knew him only through the works in Tanguy's shop.

'He was dressed,' wrote Bernard, 'in a long cloak and had a sort of game-bag at his side; his movements were painfully slow and he stooped. I walked up to him and asked him if I might speak to M. Paul Cézanne; for, although I felt fairly sure that it was my old mentor, I was uncertain about the likeness to Pissarro's portrait. He took a step back, drew himself up, took off his hat with a flourish, revealing a bald

119 *La Colline des Pauvres* 1888–94

head and the face of an old general, and said: "Here he is: what do you want of him?"'

In 1894, Emile Bernard had left France for Italy and then Egypt, where he had stayed for ten years. Arriving at Marseilles in 1904 with his wife and two children, he had wanted to visit the painter he so much admired. He received such a warm welcome that he stayed in Aix for a whole month. The two men could not see enough of each other: Cézanne because he felt that Bernard understood and admired him; Bernard because he wanted to 'learn something from a man who knows so much'.

120   *The Viaduct*   1898–1902

121   *Bridge and Pool*   1888–90

We owe our knowledge of Cézanne's ideas and pictorial technique largely to the friendship which sprang up between these two men. Cézanne was delighted to be able to expound his beliefs and give a teacher's advice to his pupil, subsequently defining his ideas more precisely by letter to Bernard. Bernard took care to note everything down so as to learn from it, and to share it with others later. He published Cézanne's letters to him, and they have become invaluable documents for our understanding of the 'father of modern painting'. The passion, the frenzy and the kind of fury with which the old man worked astounded Bernard. 'I began to understand his painting better,' he said. 'I had always liked it, but had not quite grasped it because I thought it exaggerated; in fact, it is unbelievably sincere and truthful.' He was equally surprised by the extreme kindness of the man described in Paris as a churlish, coarse-spoken cynic. Cézanne often went to dinner with Bernard and his family in the small flat they had rented near the theatre. He was courteous to Mme Bernard, played with the children, and chattered happily until the conversation turned to painting. Then

122   *Mont Sainte-Victoire*   1900–6

he became excited and raised his voice, drumming on the table with his fingers.

Bernard sometimes accompanied Cézanne into the countryside around Aix, to Bibémus and the Château Noir or along the Arc. On the return journey, if Cézanne was pleased with his work, he sometimes recited passages from Baudelaire and Virgil, his favourite poets, for whom he had an infallible memory. At other times, when his companion's theorizing got on his nerves, he would walk off and leave him standing in the road. After Bernard had left Aix, he tried to continue their conversations by post, but Cézanne was a little reserved about this and wrote increasingly shorter letters. In the end he became impatient with Bernard's love of abstract discussion. 'The artist,' he wrote to him, 'must guard against that literary spirit which so often leads the painter off his true path, namely the concrete study of nature, and makes him lose his way for too long in intangible speculations. Literature expresses itself by abstractions, whereas painting, by means of outline and colour, gives concrete shape to sensations and perceptions. . . . Don't be an art critic! Just paint, and you will be safe.'

In his last letter to Bernard, written on 21 September 1906, Cézanne appears to be avoiding questions which obviously must have been too demanding. 'I notice,' he wrote, 'that I never give you a straight answer. You will have to forgive me; the reason, as I have already told you, is that I am constantly concerned about the goal I hope to achieve. I still study nature and seem to be making slow progress. I would like to have you here, for my loneliness weighs on me a little. But I am old and sick and I have sworn to die painting.' A month later, almost to the day, he did, in fact, die painting.

123　　*The Gardener*　1900–6

I have made some progress, but why so painfully and so late? Is art perhaps a kind of priest-
hood, demanding complete self-sacrifice?
CÉZANNE TO VOLLARD, 9 January 1903

The conflict of mind and senses

Despite his physical decline, Cézanne maintained, right up to his death, a surprising lucidity and ability to work. His late success did not alter his way of life any more than his early difficulties and disappointments had done: nothing distracted him from his sole concern, the 'realization' of his work. He found himself sought after by collectors and foreign museums, and invited to take part in important exhibitions; yet not a word of satisfaction or pride escaped his lips. In 1904, the Salon d'Automne, which had been founded the preceding year, devoted an entire room to him. Camille Mauclair wrote in *La Revue Bleue*: 'It's the most incoherent nonsense anyone could have dreamt up, phoney, brutal and mad. Cézanne's name will be associated with the most unforgettable joke in art in the last fifteen years.' Other critics accused him of being a charlatan and an imbecile. The thirty-three canvases exhibited were, however, received with enthusiasm by one segment of the press, notably the younger artists. Jean Puy, in an article in *Le Mercure de France*, wrote: 'Thanks to him, Impressionism has been brought back to the paths of tradition and logic. His teaching is immense.' The *Mémorial d'Aix* reprinted this comment, and added: 'Too little understood in Aix, or, rather, too often misunderstood, we congratulate this painter on his success.' Cézanne reacted to these eulogies with his usual irreverence: 'The intellectuals of my homeland are a bunch of illiterate cretins and rascals.'

Also in 1904, he exhibited for the second time at the Libre Esthétique in Brussels. In the following year, he was invited to show at the Salon des Indépendants and, again, at the Salon d'Automne, where he was represented by ten paintings. His admirers came to Aix to see him: the painters Maurice Denis, Charles Camoin, K.-X. Roussel and Hermann-Paul, and the critics Francis Jourdain, R.-P. Rivière and J.-F. Schnerb. The dealers Vollard, G. Bernheim-Jeune and Durand-Ruel began to court him. He treated all these people with politeness, but also with suspicion. He was annoyed that his works were being haggled over. 'There's no escaping people's trickery,' he said; 'it's all a matter of robbery, vanity, infatuation, rape and someone grabbing one's work.' At this point, he entrusted his son with the management of his affairs.

He took little care of himself, and his diabetes grew worse. He suffered from vertigo and violent headaches, and had difficulty in walking. Since he was no longer able to lunch in the rue Boulegon, Mme Brémond had to bring his meals to the summer-house of Les Lauves. When he wanted to paint out of doors, he had his coachman drive him to the banks of the Arc, or the Trois-Sautets bridge, or the chemin des Milles. Once there, he did not have to walk far before discovering 'that magnificent richness of colour which gives life to nature. Here on the river bank,' he added, 'there are endless themes, for one subject may be viewed from different angles, each of which provides a more interesting study than the last. They are all so varied that I think I could work here for months without moving, except to tilt my head a little to the right and then a little to the left.'

Cézanne had reached the greatest point in his life, where joy and suffering merged so closely that they could no longer affect his strength of purpose, where he was fully aware of his powers and his limitations. This is not to say, however, that, in the sheer joy of painting, he became uncritical, or that old age made him rash. Civilized people need the reassurance of intangible laws, applicable in all times and circumstances: in Uccello it is linear perspective; in Rembrandt, his chiaroscuro. Thus it is disconcerting to be faced with a painter who is searching in chaos for a new order, who is trying to replace accepted traditions by new ones. Each of Cézanne's paintings shows signs of his search, through change, instability and the contradictions in the world and his own personality, for the pictorial absolute. Unlike Da Vinci, Holbein or Ingres, who are marked by the certainty of their approach to painting, masters such as El Greco, Velasquez and Delacroix are prey to anxiety and anguish as they struggle to express their ideals. These feelings Cézanne also experienced, in proportion to his genius.

It is not particularly helpful to divide Cézanne's career into romantic, Impressionist, analytic, synthetic and baroque periods as Lionello Venturi and other art historians have done, for all these periods merge

124 *Mont Sainte-Victoire* 1904–6

into one stream which carried the artist ever nearer unattainable perfection. However tremendous his inspiration or impetuous his brush strokes, his last paintings are as firmly constructed as those of his maturity. In this later period, the controlling outlines, the geometric structure of the objects and the unity of the composition are hidden by a liveliness, almost a violence, which Cézanne was justified in using because it implied an assurance gained by years of thought, experimentation and patient, methodical work. As noted, it was in 1904 that Cézanne, in the middle of his so-called 'baroque' period, advised Emile Bernard to 'see in nature the cylinder, the sphere, the cone', adding that 'nature, for us, is more depth than surface . . . To penetrate what is in front of you and persist in trying to express it as logically as possible.'

Cézanne's life was a steady progression towards the ultimate moment of perfect possession. Each of his works represents a step forward. Let us examine some of the sixty paintings which he did, between 1882 and 1906, of the same landscape. In the *Mont Sainte-Victoire* of the Metropolitan Museum, New York (1885–7), he is concerned with depicting every element of the scene in front of him: the irregularities of the land, the trees, the houses, the arches of a viaduct. He exercises complete freedom of interpretation. He constructs a conventional but tense and highly concentrated landscape by means of nervous, dense and violent splashes of colour. Other works give the same impression, notably the *Sainte-Victoire* in Philadelphia, the one in Basel and the one in the Pushkin Museum, which is the last one he did. It applies, in fact, to all those which he painted from the chemin des Lauves between 1904 and 1906. Emotional and at the same time stable, they are the most lyrical of all the paintings he did of his beloved mountain. They possess a feeling of exaltation which, whatever critics may have said, has nothing in common with the pantheism of Chinese painting, for Cézanne's works are a complex of broken features, jagged forms and dramatic contrasts between the greens and oranges and the blues and violets. All the material of nature is reversed. Everything appears to be displaced: the warm tones are pushed into the background, the cold ones are moved to the fore, and the denser parts of the painting are illogically distributed. And

Ills. 122, 125, 126

125   *Sainte-Victoire*   1905–6

126   *Sainte-Victoire*   1904–6

while the transfigured mountain advances towards us, the sky and the open countryside are swept along by an impetuous movement whose vibrations spread in all directions. Out of the chaos, however, a spatial harmony and an overriding balance emerge, due to the shimmering quality of the light and air. This chaos is the image of the primeval disorder with which Cézanne identified himself. 'I breathe the virginity of the world,' he said. 'An acute awareness of colour torments me. I feel myself washed by all the colours of infinity. I become one with my painting. We live in a rainbow chaos. I stand in front of my subject, lose myself in it. I dream, hazily. The sun, like a distant friend, secretly warms my idleness and makes it fruitful. We germinate.'

Ill. 127
From *Boy in a Red Waistcoat* (1890–5) and *Man with a Pipe* (1892, Courtauld Institute) to the *Portrait of Vallier* (1906, Leigh Block Collection, Chicago), Cézanne's figures, too, show a marked lyricism, which is expressed by a greater flexibility and delicate modulations that conceal the bone structure of the model. The *Portrait of Joachim Gasquet* (1896, National Gallery, Prague) is constructed with the aid of striking *Ills. 116,* contrasts of planes and colours. In *The Watchmaker* (1895–1900, Gug-*128* genheim Museum, New York) and *Self-Portrait with Béret* (1898–1900, Robert Treat Paine Collection, Boston), the lines are already less rigid, and the colour transitions more gradual. As for Cézanne's last portraits, such as *The Young Italian Girl* (1896, Harry Bakwin Collection, *Ills. 129,* New York), *Old Woman with Rosary* (1900–4, National Gallery London), *130* *Little Girl with Doll* (Academy of Arts, Honolulu) and *Woman in a Hat* (Wildenstein Collection, New York), I think it best to limit our analysis to one example.

It is obvious that the *Peasant in a Blue Smock* (1895–1900) is closer to the *Card Players,* the *Man with a Pipe* and the *Peasant* of the Hahnloser Collection (Winterthur), painted between 1890 and 1892, than to the *Old Peasant* (1900–4, formerly Vollard Collection), which expresses an emotion unusual with Cézanne. Here the massive forms are covered by a fine mesh of orange-yellow and brown joined together by a series of pinks, blues and violets. In order to bring out the simplicity and serenity of this old farm labourer, Cézanne has greatly enlarged the hands. The

127   *Portrait of Vallier*   1906

128   *The Watchmaker*   1895–1900

Portrait of Vallier – he was Cézanne's gardener – in the Lecomte Collection, and above all the one in the Leigh Block Collection in Chicago, which was the last portrait painted by Cézanne, appears in a strange light when one compares it with one of the *Card Players* or with the *Boy in a Red Waistcoat*. This bearded gardener, shown in profile and with his hands folded, is no longer an individual isolated within a solid space, but a form subjected to vibrations of the air and light, sucked into the shadows of the background. The painting is composed of moving surfaces, broken rhythms, glimmers, reflections and vanishing outlines. The features of the face are undefined, and the left hand – the only one visible – is merely sketched. The artist's attention is concentrated on the model's clothes, which are a complex of broken lines, multiple scratches and shimmering splashes of colour, giving the sitter a weightless, insubstantial character. He has been withdrawn, as a man, from the misery of his condition, and becomes simply a depersonalized element in the life of the universe.

Between 1895 and 1904, Cézanne painted about thirty still-lifes. Clearly, an inanimate object was less suited to his lyricism than a landscape. Here too, however, he exercised much greater freedom than in his early still-lifes. *Still-life with Onions and Bottle* (1896–1900, Louvre), for instance, does not vary greatly from his previous still-lifes, but the colours are applied with finer, softer brush strokes. An indefinable atmosphere unites the collection of objects piled on the table. Although, as he grew older, Cézanne continued to express the volumes and density of fruit by colour, he also felt the need to underline their depth, thereby gaining a more pleasing effect. There are now fewer plain backgrounds, and ornamentation appears in their place. He introduces a curtain behind the table more often than before, and this curtain is now covered with embroidery or floral patterns. The yellow curtain of the *Still-life* (1890–1) in the Barnes Foundation was replaced a few years later by the gaudy rumpled one of such paintings as the *Still-life with Apples* (Museum of Modern Art, New York) and *Still-life with Apples and Oranges* (Louvre). In a painting in the Bernheim-Jeune Collection (1895–1900), the exaggerated lyricism which he was usually

Ills. 132, 133

221

129   *Woman in a Hat*   1900–4

130   *Old Woman with Rosary*   1900–4

131   *Peasant*   1895–1900

able to control seems to have broken loose, and an almost unbearable violence moves across this extraordinary painting. Instead of allowing the folds in the damask hangings to fall naturally, he angrily rumples and breaks them up, dropping them heavily on to the table. And the table itself is unusual, for, besides being abnormally thick, it forms a truncated pentagon which makes use of the inverted perspective favoured by young French painters some fifty years later. This painting is a mixture of impetuosity, instability and lack of continuity. In the turmoil of broken lines, acute angles and splashes of colour, only the perfect oval of the plate and the pure spheres of the fruit give a touch of harmony and peace.

Cézanne sometimes increased the rhythm and emphasized the decorative effects of the painting, so as to avoid monotony and austerity: a tapestry embroidered with red and blue flowers replaces the white cloth and napkin which used to lie on a corner of the table, or sometimes appears in addition. The *Still-life with Tea-pot* (Davies Collection, London) and *Vase with Sugar Bowl* (Museum of Modern Art, New York) are examples of this. In the two versions of *Still-life with Cupid,* done in 1895 after a sculpture by Puget, Cézanne seems to have tried to reconcile the architectural idea with his own penchant for the baroque, to join the statue's curves with the two surrounding geometrical planes, and so to ensure the coherence of a series of perspective systems. In the painting in the National Museum in Stockholm, and even more in the one in the Courtauld Institute, he concentrated on increasing the angles of vision and creating depth by a sequence of overlapping planes, by canvases placed obliquely against the wall, by the revolving surfaces of the ground and by the rectangle of the table; he avoided vanishing lines converging on a fixed point. The two pieces of fruit on the chair are as large as those in the foreground, and the one in the far background on the floor is almost the size of a balloon. Yet, despite his continual infringement of the rules of painting, what a vivid sense of space he has created!

Cézanne now became increasingly concerned with trying to suggest the hidden unrest within an object as well as its rhythmical order. The

132   *Still-life with Apples and Oranges*   1895–1900

fruits spill out of the stand or plate on to the white cloth, and the surface of the table is brought to life by the rhythm of spherical and cylindrical shapes. This creates an impression of movement, which is heightened by the rumpling of the tapestries and curtains, and the fall of the table-cloth. The *Still-life with Apples and Oranges* (Bernheim-Jeune Collection) and *Still-life with Curtain* (Musée de l'Ermitage), both painted about 1895–1900, illustrate this. Cézanne's barely restrained romanticism gives an expressionist overtone to the strange still-lifes with skulls in the Barnes and Dueby-Mueller Collections. Paradoxically, he responds to

Ill. 103

such subjects as a bunch of flowers, which normally requires charm and delicacy, by intensifying the dramatic action. His brush seems to have been carried away by the same frenzy which shakes the *Great Pine* and makes the *Château Noir* tremble on its foundations, as may be seen in *Flowered Vase* in the Barnes Collection, *Flowers and Greenery* in the Pushkin Museum and *Vase in the Garden* (David Eccles, London). These unquiet flower paintings are quite unlike the serene *Flowers in a Delft Vase* (1873), the *Still-life with Yellow Dahlia* (1873) or *The Blue Vase* (c. 1875), all three of which are now in the Louvre.

133 *Still-life with Apples* 1895–1900

Nevertheless, Cézanne controlled his lyricism more easily in these paintings of inanimate objects than in his other works, for they gave him time to arrange his themes, plan the lighting and formal relationships, and take pains over the execution. This explains why there are fewer unfinished canvases among his still-lifes than in any other category.

134   *The Great Pine*   1892–6

135 *View of the Château Noir* 1894–6

It was his still-life painting which attracted the Cubists, and which gave rise among contemporary painters to an almost exclusive interest in the object as opposed to the landscape. It was in landscape painting that Cézanne most often gave way to his impulses, in the tortured scenes of the Bibémus quarry or those of the Château Noir, where he went so often towards the end of his life.

It would be wrong, however, to regard Cézanne at this time as an aging painter dominated by his senses. The strength of his emotions never destroyed his feeling for composition. *Maison Maria on the Road to the Château Noir* (1895–8, Pellerin Collection, Paris) and his last work,

136 *Montgeroult at Sunset* 1899

137   *Le Cabanon de Jourdan*   1906

left unfinished, *Le Cabanon de Jourdan* (1906, Kunstmuseum, Basel),   *Ill. 137*
proves the truth of Raynal's words: 'Cézanne's obsession with geometry
was unexpectedly revived at the very moment when he began to free
himself from the restrictions of his technique.' In fact, the 'obsession
with geometry' had never left him. The *Cabanon de Jourdan* and the
Maison Maria are as solidly constructed as the *Maison de Bellevue* (1890–2,
Bührle Collection), the *Jas de Bouffan* (1885–7, National Gallery, Prague)
and *Houses at L'Estaque* (1883–5, Harrison Collection, New York).
Maurice Raynal is right in saying that, 'to his dying day, Cézanne
suffered from the tyrannical conflict of mind and senses.' To this we

231

must add that Cézanne's mind was never conquered by his senses. The road to the Château Noir creates an acute angle with the masonry; the lines, the volumes and the amazing touches which give life to the land and sky are all subject to a strange obliqueness; yet the mind intervenes to restore balance in this remarkable painting.

CHAPTER TWELVE

Every time I look at a Poussin,
I know myself better.
Cézanne to Joachim Gasquet

Les Grandes Baigneuses

The 'tyrannical conflict' which disturbed Cézanne so deeply in old age came to an end in *Les Grandes Baigneuses* (Museum of Art, Philadelphia), on which he had worked for seven years, from 1898 to 1905. This huge *Ill. 139* painting, measuring 82 in. by 98 in., represents the culmination of Cézanne's research in painting techniques, as well as his spiritual last will and testament. It embodies, moreover, an unusual spatial conception. For thirty years he had been obsessed with painting the human body, but this was the first time that his diffidence and prudishness allowed him to approach the subject openly and study it in depth. He had, of course, painted numerous *Baigneurs* and *Baigneuses* before this. The human body had been a constant source of concern and anguish for him. Every adolescent desire and youthful dream, all the thoughts of a man close to death, the whole history of a soul thirsting for love yet defenceless in the face of it, a soul attracted by carnal beauty yet suspicious of it – all this is represented by the series of female nudes which culminated in *Les Grandes Baigneuses*.

The earlier paintings – notably *The Temptation of St Anthony* (1867), *A Modern Olympia* (1870), *La Lutte d'amour* (1875) and the various *Baigneurs* and *Baigneuses* in the Musée de la Ville de Paris (1880), the Dueby-Mueller Collection (1885), the Kunsthaus in Basel (1886–7), the Pushkin Museum (1890–4) and the Louvre (1890–4) – are only stages in the progression towards this monumental work. Many of the studies of bathers made by Cézanne have been destroyed. About sixty still survive, however, to prove the determination and concentration he

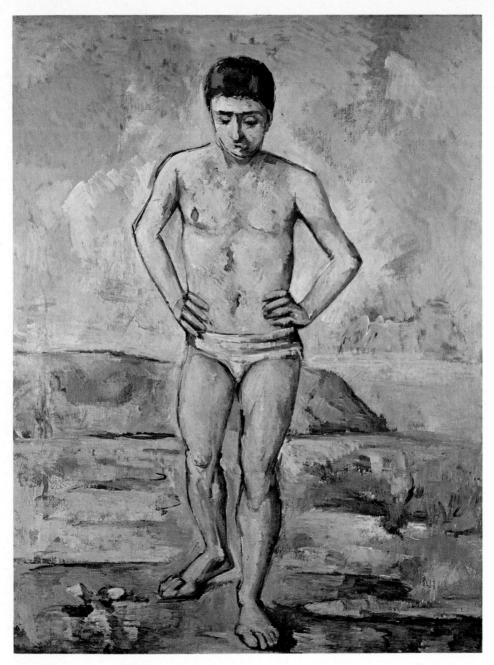

138 *Le Grand Baigneur* 1885–7

139 *Les Grandes Baigneuses* 1898–1905

applied to the preparation of the *Grandes Baigneuses* of the Philadelphia Museum and those which were done at the same time (1898–1905): namely, the *Baigneuses* in the Barnes Foundation and the one in the National Gallery, London (purchased in 1965 for £500,000 from the Pellerin family). The *Baigneuses* of the Art Institute in Chicago, the Etta Cone Collection in Baltimore and the K.-X. Roussel Collection are conceived in a different manner; they are less intellectual, less stable, and more elaborate and equivocal in construction.

Cézanne was too concerned about public opinion to have women pose for him naked. Only once, in 1894, when painting his *Female Nude* (Lecomte Collection) and the water-colour acquired by the Louvre in 1951, did he risk using a professional model. Normally he made do with illustrated magazines. On one occasion, while watching a group of young soldiers bathing, he made notes, and he came to use these extensively, even transforming men into women in some of his paintings. He also gathered information at the Louvre, making mental notes or sketches of the nudes of Titian, Veronese, Tintoretto and Rubens. 'Their flesh,' he said, 'is like a caress and has bodily warmth.' This is the voice of the romantic, sensual Cézanne. The other Cézanne, the intellectual organizer, preferred to go and meditate in front of Poussin's works, more often than not in front of the *Bacchanal*. Perhaps the brilliant arrangement of Poussin's nymphs inspired the body rhythms and pyramidal composition of the *Grandes Baigneuses*.

Ever since his youth he had admired two masters, Delacroix and Poussin; although they were opposed in temperament, each corresponded to one or the other side of Cézanne's character, the one appealing to his romanticism, and the other to his feeling for the classical. If some of his nudes are close to those of Delacroix – for example, the *Baigneur* of the Spencer Churchill Collection (1883–7), that of the Barnes Foundation (1892–4) and the water-colour *Standing Nude* in the Louvre – it is Poussin's nudes that inspired the *Grandes Baigneuses*. 'Poussin recreated entirely from nature', he said to Gasquet, 'and that's the sort of classicism I understand . . . Every time I look at a Poussin, I know myself better.' He stated this thought more precisely, again to Gasquet, as follows: 'I want to understand in order the better to feel, to feel in order the better to understand. I want to be truly classical, and to rediscover the classical approach through nature and sensation.'

Cézanne's concern, however, was not with a classicism set in the mould of conventional themes, whether these came from history, mythology or the Old Testament, nor with its obsolete traditions in linear perspective, modelling and chiaroscuro, but with a revitalized and up-to-date classicism. Although he wanted, like Poussin, to bring the human being and the landscape harmoniously together, he achieved this by means of a new language of form – the language, in fact, of the *Grandes Baigneuses,* in which the women's bodies, the trees and the clouds are inextricably joined together within a contrived space. All the elements in this masterpiece combine to give the pyramidal composition an impetus which is cut short by the upper edge of the canvas, so that the sides of the triangle formed by the trees meet only in the spectator's imagination. There is a subtle interplay of parallels in this painting: the oblique parallels of the bathers and the trees, counter parallels of the

140 *Baigneurs* 1890–1900

bather's arms and, to restore the balance, the horizontal parallels of the river and the river banks. Both the bathers and the trees are subject to the same pattern, and appear to be drawn upwards by some mysterious force. Although the outlines are clearly drawn, the branches and leaves, the ground and the sky, are only scumbles, from which issues a soft bluish light. Cézanne, a master of colour, uses only three tones in this painting, ochre, green and blue, but they are linked by intermediary shades to create a softness of atmosphere.

The depersonalization of the figures, the stability of the forms, the vibrations of the colours, the purity and grandeur of the architectonic rhythms, everything in the picture is the result of intellectual speculation and slow, carefully considered execution. It is the image of a world so perfectly conceived that it appears shut in on itself, and yet it opens up endless possibilities for escape. The spectator moves as in a dream without boundary, yet remains aware that nothing in this brilliant construction can be added or removed without destroying it. Never had Cézanne so closely linked his sensations to the great movements of nature. At last he had achieved the classicism he had sought in all his earlier great works. In the *Grandes Baigneuses*, he succeeded not only in reconciling his lyricism with his sense of composition, but also in harmonizing his mental patterns with the sensitive material of nature. The painting is a compound of richness and simplicity, freedom and rigidity, strength and delicacy. It is a work of magnificent architecture, yet woven with so delicate and exquisite a thread that it has the appearance of a sketch and was for a long time thought to be unfinished. I say 'appearance', for a masterpiece of this kind is the product of long years of reflection and technical experience. Rather, it possesses the external qualities of freshness and spontaneity to be found in a water-colour. In fact, Cézanne the watercolourist or draughtsman helps to explain Cézanne the painter, and perhaps even dominates him.

141   Cézanne with *Les Grandes Baigneuses*

142   *Still-life*   *c.* 1900

CHAPTER THIRTEEN

> His water-colours are more vibrant and
> spontaneous than his oil paintings, though
> equally truthful and at the same time more
> poetic, because freer and more suggestive.
> They completely answered the demands of
> his genius.
>
> BERNARD DORIVAL ON CÉZANNE, 1948

Draughtsman and watercolourist

Cézanne's work, when seen as a whole, shows a remarkable diversity of technique. Each of his themes is dealt with in a way which varies from one painting to the next. Cézanne himself said: 'The method of working arises from a contact with nature; it is developed according to circumstance. It entails seeking an expression of what one feels, then of organizing the feeling according to a personal aesthetic. I try to develop logically what we see and feel by studying nature, and I do not worry about the methods until later, because they are, for us, merely the means of making the public aware of what we feel, and getting them to accept it.' If we ignore his early and inevitably experimental works, and examine only his successful paintings, we find that their execution is rarely governed by the same set of rules. The strokes are in turn dense or fluid, short or long, square or thread-like, vertical or oblique, confused in thin lines or as clearly defined as the facets of a crystal. Lines may cross at right-angles or follow sinuous arabesques. As may be seen in the *Baigneuses devant la tente* (1885, R. Moltzan Collection, Oslo) and the *Baigneurs* formerly in the Gourgaud Collection (1892–4), the outline may be blurred, when the artist is expressing atmosphere, or it may be sharply defined, when he is trying to isolate form.

Natural proportions are observed in one place and ignored in another. The form is contracted, as in the *Portrait of the Artist's Son* (1885, National Gallery of Art, Washington), or elongated out of all proportion, as with the right leg of the *Harlequin* or the arm of the *Boy in a Red Waistcoat*. The hands of the *Woman in a Hat* (1900–4, Wildenstein Collection, New

York) are drawn with delicate precision; those of the *Old Peasant*, though dating from the same period, are bulky and twice their natural size. This same *Old Peasant* is painted in neutral tones only, whereas the *Dovecot at Bellevue* (1888–92), *Mont Sainte-Victoire Seen from Bibémus* (1898) and the *Cabanon de Jourdan* (1906) are soaked in orange yellow, emerald green and cobalt blue.

Having shown himself particularly sensitive to form and volume, Cézanne turned to colour for the organization of space. 'I try to render perspective solely by means of colour,' he told the collector Osthaus in 1906. In 1904, he had already said to Emile Bernard: 'Nature, for us, is more depth than surface, and hence the need to bring into our light vibrations, which are represented by reds and yellows, a sufficient quantity of bluishness to make the air felt.' For him, light was orange, shade was blue. In order to pass from orange to blue, he used modulations of violet or blue violet or, again, modulations of greenish yellow or bluish green. This done, he suggested planes by their edges and by complementary colours. Even when transforming the local tone by an interplay of shining colours and reflections, he tried to recover classical grandeur by means of a geometric outline, supporting his work on a skeleton of vertical and horizontal lines, counterbalanced by oblique ones. Finally, rather than resort to traditional perspective, he approached the object from several viewpoints. The first Cubists were not to forget this.

No matter what perspective method he chose, never, even when his lyricism was at its height, did Cézanne neglect firmness of structure, *Ill. 135* solidity of composition. Even such a powerful painting as the *Château Noir* in the Oskar Reinhart Collection, in which forms and tones are highly fragmented, is controlled by a hidden geometry. Charles Bouleau, the author of *Charpentes*, has shown that the *Château Noir* is held within a framework of right-angled strips which divide the surface area into five vertical and three horizontal bands, severed by oblique parallels that determine the rectangles, squares and rhombs – a system which was to be fully developed in the *Grandes Baigneuses*. Bouleau goes on to say: 'Cézanne, however, never expressed depth by means of geometry, nor

143   *Boy in a Red Waistcoat*   1890–5

ever made direct use of the diagonals of a rectangle to create depth.' The idea that, at a given moment, Cézanne freed himself from his former emphasis on structure in order to give way to his romantic impulses is such a common misconception that we must do our utmost to set the matter straight.

Cézanne's life was fraught with doubts and anxieties, and he had to fight constantly in order to overcome them. His letters and his sayings are eloquent: 'I cannot express myself . . . I lack fulfilment . . . I am too old. I have not fulfilled myself and I shall not do so now . . . I am like someone who owns a piece of gold and can do nothing with it . . . I shall not have enough time to express myself. To work!' And work, relentless work, was Cézanne's life. He worked when he was at the height of his powers, and he worked with even more intensity when they began to ebb. 'With each touch,' he cried, 'I am risking my life!' And the older he grew the more he wanted to avenge himself for all the misunderstandings, injustices and humiliations to which he had been subjected. Ingres' bitter remark, 'I am counting on my old age; it will avenge me,' might well have been made by Cézanne.

We know how painful his work was, how he abandoned paintings and then began work on them again after months, even years, how he made several versions of a picture and began portraits he never finished. Then there were many canvases which he destroyed in a moment of anger or depression, or left behind in a studio, flat or hotel room. Yet this instability never destroyed his patience, and he allowed neither his disappointments nor his despair to interfere with his daily work. Self-taught, he had only himself to depend on: in overcoming his ignorance, deepening his vision and learning to master his language by experience. He had to bear the perils of the undertaking on which he had embarked and to find his own means to bring it to fruition. He had to press on continually because he knew that even the slightest pause would be a regression. Cézanne's entire work is the story of the conquest of genius by patience and deliberation. The process involved him in suffering because his personality was too demanding for him not to wish to free himself from the limitations of technique.

The knowledge we acquire sustains and enslaves us at the same time. Cézanne, more than any other, felt that he needed a long sequence of experiments, trials and failures before he could attain the final mastery, or even the *facility*, in the best sense of the word, which he privately envied in certain of his contemporaries. His remarks about other painters, though sometimes veiled in sarcasm, are revealing: of Delacroix he said, 'He still has the most beautiful palette in France'; of Courbet, 'A crude plasterer but there is no one to surpass him'; and of Renoir, 'A craftsman . . . a great talent'. And it is not without hidden admiration that he said of Manet, whom he disliked, 'He spews out the tones . . . I would have liked to paint with the whole palette as he does, but I could not, so now I paint as I can.' Zola wrote to a disheartened Cézanne, 'And you, who have the spark of genius, something which can never be acquired, you complain, when all you have to do to succeed is use your fingers and work like a craftsman.' And Cézanne replied, 'I am heavy, stupid and slow.'

At the time he made this remark, Cézanne was still working in a dark and cloying style with the impetuosity, but also the strength, of a highly gifted adolescent. However, although his oil paintings were heavy and uncertain, his drawings and his water-colours, the first of which were done at this time, show him already capable of great spontaneity and clarity. The sketches he scribbled in the margins of his letters to Zola possess these qualities, as does a water-colour of 1865, *Près d'Aix*, in the collection of his son. Right up to his death, Cézanne continued to do drawings and water-colours which are often more successful than his oil paintings. His drawings (both in pencil and in water-colour) were not so much preparatory sketches and studies for paintings as a means of fixing on paper the initial sensation and preserving it whole. Often, in fact, a painting of a subject was done at the same time as the water-colour, or even before it. Each, then, water-colour and oil painting, is an independent work in its own right. It is notable that the paintings Cézanne did during the last twenty years of his life remind one of water-colours in their lightness of touch and delicate colouring. Indeed, there are many similarities between the two: the unpainted sections of the canvas, the transparency of the shadows, the lack of continuity in the coloured patches, instability of form and light, fluidity of atmosphere and that liveliness which gives the brush strokes the appearance of having been guided more by pure feeling than by the material demands of the medium.

Some of the many paintings bearing a resemblance to water-colours are *Self-portrait with Palette* (1885–7), *Madame Cézanne in the Garden* (1880–2, Walter Collection), *Portrait of Madame Cézanne* (1885, Max Moos Collection, Geneva), *The Great Pine* (1892–6, São Paulo Museum), *Country Road* (1900–6, Staatsgalerie, Munich), certain scenes of Bibémus, the Château Noir and Mont Sainte-Victoire and important sections of the *Baigneurs* and *Baigneuses*. Cézanne appears, in all his works, to have been irresistibly drawn to improvisation, for which the technique of water-colour was better suited than any other. There is a marked contrast between his oil paintings, which are carefully planned and executed, and the water-colours, which required the sharpness of an immediate impression, rapid decisions and a sure hand, and which allowed a freedom of interpretation especially suited to his temperament. It is therefore not surprising that towards the end of his life he did almost more water-colours than oil paintings, and that these were often superior to the paintings. Let us take a few examples.

Of two self-portraits done in 1894 in which Cézanne is depicted three-quarter face, the oil painting in the Pellerin Collection is not as good as the water-colour in the Walter Feilchenfeld Collection in Zürich. In the *Card Player* (1890–2) of the Chauncey McCormick Collection, Chicago (who had already appeared as one of the figures in the *Players* of the Stephen C. Clark Collection), only a few touches of dark blue and ochre were needed to create a complex of volumes that is wonderfully balanced in its simplicity. There are no modulations or shaded values, no irregularities; nothing, in fact, in this remarkable water-colour disturbs its freedom and harmony. The same is true of the *Old Peasant* (Kunsthaus, Zürich), a water-colour which Cézanne painted some ten years later, during his most energetic period. The same figure in the corresponding oil painting is executed with a number

144 *Female Nude* c. 1895

of shaded tones which soften and weaken the forms. Similarly, I prefer the water-colours to the oil paintings in the cases of the *Gardener* (1900–6, Tate Gallery) and the *Portrait of Vallier* (1906, Leigh Block Collection); and *Female Nude* (1895, formerly Pellerin Collection) is without question inferior to the highly expressive pencil drawing and to the water-colour (purchased by the Louvre in 1951), whose power of surprise has been equalled only by Picasso.

I would willingly exchange all the paintings entitled *Rocks at Bibémus* (1898) – notably those in museums in Essen, Zürich and Baltimore and in the C. Sullivan Collection in New York – for their corresponding water-colours. Similarly, many modern critics consider the water-colours of Mont Sainte-Victoire even more moving than the oil paintings on the same theme. One may admire *Great Pine at Mont Sainte-Victoire* (1883–7, formerly in the collection of Cézanne's son), or the *Sainte-Victoire* paintings done between 1890 and 1906 which are now in the Courtauld Institute, the Kunsthaus in Zürich, the Barnes Foundation, the Louvre and several private collections; but it is in the water-colours that the eye, which is allowed to move freely, is able to unite the separate elements, yet keep each in its rightful place. These water-colours are a mixture of elisions, ellipses, pauses and repetitions; nothing is still or heavy. One marvels at the delicacy of the tones, the way the light is created by the white space on the paper, the unreal clarity of the atmosphere and the agility with which the brush interrupts its stroke to delineate the form by a hard edge or a fleeting touch of colour. Fullness achieved through emptiness, balance through imbalance, continuity through discontinuity: the laxity of the south has been transformed into the conciseness of Japan.

Sometimes, however, the baroque in Cézanne's character came to the surface. At the same time as he was constructing the powerful architecture of the *Grandes Baigneuses,* he was imparting a wild impetus to the *Baigneuses* in the Art Institute of Chicago. Those with a taste for the baroque may prefer the water-colours, such as the *Baigneuses* in the Bührle (Zürich) and Oppenheim (Berlin) Collections, and above all the one in the Aline Gobert (Fontainebleau) Collection, where

145 *Mont Sainte-Victoire* 1883–7

a gust of wind seems to have tossed the bodies one against the other, and jumbled them together with the ruffled leaves of the trees. Beneath this agitated rhythm, however, one glimpses a controlling intelligence forever on the alert. In any case, these water-colours have an intrinsic value and are ends in themselves, not mere preparatory studies.

Cézanne also made drawings and water-colours of still-lifes. Familiar objects such as fruit and flowers seem to lose their material consistence, while still preserving their density and brilliance. And here again he uses, with great facility, the white surface of the paper to concentrate the light on the side of a bottle, on the curve of a fruit or on the precise point around which the spatial elements are articulated. This is especially true of the still-lifes drawn or painted between 1900 and 1906, notably the water-colours in the Ford and Seligmann Collections, as well as the *Apples on a Sideboard* and *Chair, Bottle and Apples* of the Courtauld

Institute, in which Cézanne's remark to Emile Bernard that 'design and colour are not separate things' is clearly illustrated.

Let us now examine two still-lifes executed about 1885 on the same subject, *Flowers and Fruit*, the one an oil painting in the Art Institute of Chicago, and the other a water-colour in the Paul M. Hirschland Collection, New York. The first, by its simplicity and unaffected realism, belongs to the tradition of Linard, Chardin and Courbet. The second possesses a remarkable freedom in the brush work, whose boldness almost divides colour from form. Everything in this

146   *The Dessert*   1900–6

147 *The Pitcher* 1885–95

work is allusive, barely expressed, and appears to have been improvised. In the base, leaves and flowers, a few touches of yellow, ochre, purple, blue grey and purple grey, hurriedly painted on to the white of the paper, are enough to convey the fragile beauty of the subject. There are no outlines, no continuous lines, no intermediary hues, no ethereal relationships or delicate washes, and yet the work achieves overall cohesion.

There are many studies, principally of roses, in which Cézanne demonstrates an unexpected sense of fantasy, an easy unconcern; at

148   *Still-life with Flowers and Fruit*   1890–4

times he displays a *brio* which one would not have suspected in a painter who so much distrusted this quality. His draughtsman's vision, however, is usually more profound, more severe. For instance, in *The Skull* (formerly Ambroise Vollard Collection) and *Garment Left on a Chair* (Feilchenfeldt Collection, Zürich), two water-colours of 1890–1900, he achieves an extraordinary intensity of expression. Only in Van Gogh's *Shoes* have I seen anything so touching as this everyday garment carelessly abandoned on a chair, still swollen with its owner's presence, imbued with a wholly human life. The collar at the top, the crumpling

Ills. 150, 151

of the folds and the fall of the sleeves, indeed the entire garment, are treated exactly like Mont Sainte-Victoire. Similarities of this kind are common in Cézanne's work. By studying nature, he came to understand it and to reach to its heart.

This kind of active meditation, which enabled him to reach the great universal rhythms beneath the surface of objects, inspired him to do drawings which show remarkable analytical strength and poetic abstraction. In the studies of trees and undergrowth which he made at Pontoise, Auvers, Fontainebleau, Chantilly and Médan, and in Savoy and Provence, he achieves remarkable conciseness of expression.

149   *Rose in a Green Vase*   1885–95

150   *Study of a Skull*   1895–1900

Notable examples are three water-colours dating from 1895–1900 –
Trees in the Wind, Pine-trees at Bibémus (Sullivan Collection, New
York) and *Bare Trees at the Water's Edge* (H.M. Remarque Collection)
– and the two series *Les Arbres en X* (1888), one version of which belongs
to Oskar Reinhart, and *Les Arbres en V* (1890–8), a version of which
is owned by Princess Bassiano. This last is the ultimate creation of a
mind skilled in rejecting useless digressions and concentrating on the
essential. Whereas Cézanne's oil paintings often seem to be trapped by
the density of the material, his graphic works portraying the same
themes have freed themselves from the laws of weight and the pains
or arduous work. Neither the *Road at Chantilly* (1888) in the Chester
Beatty Collection nor the one in the David M. Lévy Collection has
the fluidity, brevity or startling construction of its corresponding

Ills. 152,
153, 154,
155

254

151   *Garment Left on a Chair*   1890–1900

152   *Trees in the Wind*   1895–1900

water-colour (Museum of Modern Art, New York, and formerly Bernheim-Jeune Collection respectively). The same applies to the *Chestnut Trees at the Jas de Bouffan*, which inspired Cézanne a great many times, and the wonderful series of water-colours of Mont Sainte-Victoire, in which Cézanne conveys the rhythms of life with an amazingly light and sure hand.

Cézanne's drawings and water-colours are, to a certain extent, a refutation of his oil paintings. One of the few people to have understood this is Fernand Léger: 'Cézanne taught me love of form and volume, and the importance of drawing,' he said. 'I realized that for him a drawing had to be severe and restrained.' Faced with Cézanne's drawings, which are elliptical, freely expressed and independent of material reality, one might question his self-professed admiration for naturalism and the 'art in the museums'; indeed, one might question

153 *Pine-trees at Bibémus* 1895–1900

154 *Arbres en V* 1890–8

155 *Arbres en X* 1888–97

in general his statements on the painter's obligation to respect nature and never to lose touch with it. When he drew, he largely ignored the advice he gave to others and meant to follow himself. The 'slight shock' which he was unable, so he said, to create in his painting was the guiding power behind his drawings, in which he had already achieved what he had failed to achieve as a painter. Cézanne's power to surprise, however, should not be confused with the harsh impressionism of someone like Monet, who transforms everyday reality into a haze of images and embellishes it with glittering ornaments. Monet was not a draughtsman like Cézanne, who could strip objects of their external disguises and with one movement reach the heart of true reality. As he grew older he became more concise, quicker to unite architectonic strength with the poetry of emotion. In the end, his forms became forces, his tones a condensation of vapours, and the composition was stripped down to bare essentials.

156   *Road with a Lamp-post*   1892–4

Freed of encumbrances, Cézanne's drawings and water-colours give a haunting impression of the very essence of reality, but of a reality far removed from the visible one. Two tree trunks, for instance, may be used to represent a whole forest; a few spots of colour, scattered over the paper like a cloud of pollen, are enough to suggest a bunch of flowers. A few scratches and hard edges are all that is needed to determine volume or indicate a figure. It is a mode of expression that has much in common with the art of the Far East. Cézanne, by spending days alone in thought, with nothing but trees, brushwood and rocks for company, acquired that sharp eye and that ability to commune with inanimate objects which Chinese and Japanese painters put to such magnificent use. Thanks to the technique of drawing and water-colour (which, though more pliable, is also more demanding because it allows

157   *Forest Road*   1895–1900

of no corrections), Cézanne, who thought that he had created an image of reality, had in fact done something quite different. Far from clinging to reality for its own sake and trying to create an illusion of it, he gave it the form that his own mind had devised. A pine tree of the Château Noir is convincing because it immediately makes one think of the sap; an apple epitomizes the mutations of bud and flower. His *Card Players* and *Man with a Pipe* are concrete symbols of the hard life of the peasant, and Mont Sainte-Victoire is less a feature of the land than a violent upthrust of mysterious natural forces.

There are other similarities between Cézanne and Oriental painters, the 'flick of the wrist' and the 'scribbles' for example, and that supreme confidence which allowed him, it seems, to complete a work at one

158   *The Bank of a Stream*   1890–1900

159   *Smoker Leaning on His Elbow*   1895–1900

160   *Seated Figure: Study after Michelangelo*

go, as though his long and hard apprenticeship had given his fingers magic powers. In his oil paintings, Cézanne often appears to be trying to dissociate himself from a world burdened with an inescapable heaviness, the heaviness of coarse and rebellious material. In his drawings and water-colours, by contrast, he matches his style to the effervescent activity of living forms. The outline with its thick and narrow brush strokes, the delineation of volume, the vibrant patches of colour which divide the tranquil interstices in the background, the discovery of hidden truth – everything throbs with life and draws us into immediate and unresisting participation.

Cézanne's case is not unique. The same applies, for instance, to the artists of the eighteenth century: although their paintings were conventional, their drawings sang. Similarly, many of Delacroix's admirers prefer the nervous charm of his sketches and water-colours to the more ambitious paintings. The full genius of Daumier and Toulouse-Lautrec, perhaps also Van Gogh, is to be found in their graphic work.

161 The studio at Les Lauves

CHAPTER FOURTEEN

I am too old and I came too soon, but I mark
the way and others will follow.

CÉZANNE TO JOACHIM GASQUET

The pathfinder

If to 'realize' meant for Cézanne to eternalize the fleeting awareness
of life by the most fitting expression, or to find an adequate medium
for rendering the whole range of forms and the inner magic of the
world, if, in short, it meant achieving a coherent personal style, then
he was unaware that he had come closest to it in his drawings and
water-colours. He possessed a technique so well adapted to express
the delicacy of his perception that many of his water-colours look like
pen-and-wash drawings. When he tortured himself with his inability
to 'realize', he must have been thinking of his oil paintings. It is worth
noting that other painters, contemporaries of Cézanne, suffered in
the same way. Gauguin and Van Gogh, at the end of their careers,
expressed their sense of failure in terms almost identical with those of
Cézanne, when he said, 'I am too old and I came too soon, but I mark
the way and others will follow.'

In all the many canvases he destroyed or left unfinished, Cézanne
was, of course, seeking the impossible, the unattainable, which he
could never have found in his own time, but which those who came
after him would achieve by following in his footsteps. And he was
fully aware of this. 'My painting belongs to your generation rather than
to mine,' he said to Joachim Gasquet; 'I am the first to tread the road that
I have discovered.' But he was too stubborn and too wholly intent on
perfection to resign himself to his pioneering rôle. This was Cézanne's
tragedy, and a far crueller one than the continual struggle between the
baroque and the classical in his nature.

267

162   Cézanne at Aix in 1906

It was the Cubists who, by applying his tenets to their own doctrine, carried Cézanne's purpose to its logical conclusion. It is they who were really able to 'see in nature the cylinder, the sphere, the cone', and to develop, systematically, perhaps the greatest discovery made by any painter since Paolo Uccello. They also benefited from the contrasting planes advocated by Cézanne and, in order to emphasize them, were not afraid of breaking up or dislocating the objects in the painting. They exploited, in fact, every opportunity that Cézanne's methods offered and did not hesitate to separate the volumes and reduce the component parts of an object on the surface of the canvas. Cézanne was thus the father of Cubism, and also of those painters like Malévitch and Mondrian who were to develop Cubism into totally abstract painting. Cézanne's remark that 'the edges of an object vanish towards a point on the observer's horizon' revealed to Robert Delaunay the meaning of his research. Delaunay was also one of those who, by following Cézanne's example, tried to express depth by the use of colour – an example which was later to be exploited with great energy by Matisse and the Fauves.

All the great modern painters have been influenced by Cézanne, even those who least resemble him. 'I sometimes wonder,' said Fernand Léger, 'what would have become of modern painting without Cézanne' – and he spoke for all his generation. With the exception of the surrealists, there is no painter in the first half of this century who has not turned to Cézanne as a source of inspiration for every new experiment. Once this great revolutionary had gone, artists suddenly found themselves faced with all sorts of problems: some with the problem of geometrical construction, others with that of depth, still others with the creation of space and form by pure tones, and all of them with the intellectual transposition of the reality of the senses. 'I mark the way and others will follow.' Those who followed not only made use of his discoveries but extended their applications. Cézanne's only ambition was to express, as fully as possible, the outside world; he wanted to 'redo Poussin from nature'. For modern painters, the situation was totally different. One of them, Léon Gischia, was well aware of this, for he had himself lived through the change. 'Painting, from Van Eyck to Cézanne,' he wrote, 'is a *whole*. It is, above all, an imitative art. Cézanne questioned the method, not the principle: he was always concerned with expressing nature as completely as possible, whereas the modern painter questions the very principle itself. It is no longer a matter of providing the spectator with a more or less convincing representation of visible reality, but of replacing it with a new reality invented by

163　Interior of Cézanne's studio at Aix

the artist.' Nevertheless, if the modern painter has managed to escape from restricting imitative formulas and conventional rules, he has to admit that he owes his liberation to Cézanne.

His life ended as he had wished: he died painting. On 15 October 1906, in spite of the alarming progress of his diabetes, he went to work on the road to Tholonet. A storm blew up and it began to rain, but he carried on painting. Finally, too wet to continue, he decided to pack up his equipment and go home. Suddenly, he collapsed on the side of the road and went into a coma. He was discovered some time later by the driver of a passing carriage, who picked him up and carried him home to the rue Boulegon. Mme Brémond at once sent for a doctor, but Cézanne recovered consciousness and refused to admit that he was ill. The following day, he set out for his studio in Les Lauves to finish *Le Cabanon de Jourdan*, his last painting, but he had over-estimated his strength and, shaking with fever, barely managed to get back to the rue Boulegon. He retired to bed, this time for good. Pneumonia set in. On 20 October, Marie, who had arrived by this time, realizing he could not live long, sent word to his son. Paul failed to reply and so, on the 22nd, Mme Brémond sent him a telegram. It was Hortense who opened it, and since she had made arrangements for a dress fitting, she hid it in a drawer. Mme Brémond recalled that, during his last hours, Cézanne never ceased to watch the door for his son, but when Paul and his mother finally arrived in Aix, it was already too late. Cézanne died on 22 October. He is buried in the cemetery of his home town.

Select bibliography

The fundamental work of reference in any study of Cézanne is Lionello Venturi's *Cézanne: Son art, son oeuvre* (Paris 1936), which contains a *catalogue raisonné* of the 1,634 paintings and drawings indexed by the author. For a knowledge of Cézanne himself, the *Letters* edited by John Rewald (Paris 1937, London 1941) are indispensable, and some memoirs and reminiscences are also helpful, notably the following:

BERNARD, Emile *Souvenirs sur Paul Cézanne* (Paris 1925)
GASQUET, Joachim *Cézanne* (Paris 1921)
LARGUIER, Léo *Le Dimanche avec Paul Cézanne* (Paris 1925)
MOORE, George *Reminiscences of the Impressionist Painters* (Dublin 1906)
PISSARRO, Camille *Lettres à son fils Lucien* (New York 1943, London 1944)
VOLLARD, Ambroise *Paul Cézanne: His Life and Art* (New York 1926)
——— *En écoutant Cézanne, Degas, Renoir* (Paris 1938)
——— *Recollections of a Picture Dealer* (Boston 1936)

MONOGRAPHS AND CRITICAL STUDIES

AUZAS, P. M. *Peintures de Paul Cézanne* (Paris 1945)
BADT, Kurt *Die Kunst Cézannes* (Munich 1956)
BARNES, A. C. and de Mazia, V., *The Art of Cézanne* (New York and Paris 1939)
BERTHOLD, G. *Cézanne und die alten Meister* (Stuttgart 1958)
BOULEAU, Charles *La Géometrie secrète des peintres* (Paris 1963)
BRION-GUERRY, Liliane *Cézanne et l'expression de l'espace* (Paris 1950)
COGNIAT, Raymond *Cézanne* (Paris 1939)
COQUIOT, Gustave *Paul Cézanne* (Paris 1919)
DORIVAL, Bernard *Cézanne* (New York 1948)
FAURE, Elie *Paul Cézanne* (Paris 1936)
FEGERS, Hans *N. von Marées und P. Cézanne* (Stuttgart 1960)
FEIST, Peter H. *Paul Cézanne* (Leipzig 1963)
FELL, H. Granville *Cézanne: A Pioneer of Modern Painting* (London and Edinburgh n.d. [1933])

FRY, Roger *The French Post-Impressionists*. Preface to the catalogue of the Second Post-Impressionist Exhibition. Grafton Galleries, London 1912 (reprinted New York 1956)

——— *Cézanne: A Study of His Development* (London and New York 1927)

HUYGHE, René *Cézanne* (Paris 1936)

JEWELL, E. A. *Cézanne* (New York 1944)

JOURDAIN, Francis *Cézanne* (Paris 1950)

LHOTE, André *Cézanne* (Lausanne 1949)

MACK, Gerstle *Paul Cézanne* (New York 1935)

MEIER-GRAEFE, Julius *Cézanne* (London and New York 1927)

NEUMEYER, Alfred *Cézanne Drawings* (New York 1958)

NOVOTNY, Fritz *Cézanne* (Vienna and New York 1937)

PERRUCHOT, Henri *La Vie de Cézanne* (Paris 1958)

PFISTER, Kurt *Cézanne: Gestalt, Werk, Mythos* (Potsdam 1927)

RAYNAL, Maurice *Cézanne* (Paris 1936, Geneva 1954)

REWALD, John *Paul Cézanne* (New York 1948)

——— *The History of Impressionism* (New York 1961)

RILKE, Rainer Maria *Lettres sur Cézanne* (Paris 1944)

RIVIÈRE, Georges *Le Maître Paul Cézanne* (Paris 1923)

ROBBINS, D. *Cézanne and Structure in Modern Painting* (New York 1963)

SCHAPIRO, Meyer *Cézanne* (London and New York 1952)

SELDMAYR, Hans *Verlust der Mitte* (Salzburg 1948)

SHERMAN, H. L. *Cézanne and Visual Form* (Columbus, Ohio, 1952)

STOLL, Robert T. *Van Gogh, Gauguin, Cézanne* (Zürich 1960)

VENTURI, Lionello *Cézanne: Water Colours* (London 1934)

WALDVOGEL, Melvin *The Bathers of P. Cézanne* (Cambridge, Mass., 1961)

List of illustrations

17 *Portrait of Boyer with a Straw Hat* (*Portrait de Boyer au chapeau de paille*), 1870–1. Oil on canvas, $21\frac{5}{8} \times 15\frac{3}{8}$ in., 55×39 cm. Metropolitan Museum of Art, New York

18 *Portrait of the Negro Scipio* (*Portrait du nègre Scipion*), 1865–8. Oil on canvas, $42 \times 33\frac{1}{2}$ in., 107×83 cm. Museu de Arte, São Paulo

19 *The Black Clock* (*La Pendule en marbre noir*), 1869–71. Oil on canvas, $21\frac{1}{4} \times 28\frac{3}{4}$ in., 54×73 cm. Niarchos Collection, Paris

20 *Paul Alexis Reading a Manuscript to Zola* (*Paul Alexis lisant à Emile Zola*), 1869–70. Oil on canvas, $51\frac{1}{8} \times 63$ in., 131×161 cm. Museu de Arte, São Paulo

21 *Le Grog au vin* or *Afternoon in Naples* (*L'Après-midi à Naples*), 1866–7. Oil on canvas, $14\frac{1}{2} \times 17\frac{3}{4}$ in., 37×45 cm. Pellerin Collection, Paris

22 *Portrait of Valabrègue* (*Portrait de Valabrègue*), *c.* 1866. Oil on canvas, $45\frac{5}{8} \times 38\frac{5}{8}$ in., 116×98 cm. Wildenstein Collection, New York

23 *A Modern Olympia* (*Une Moderne Olympia*), 1872–3. Oil on canvas, $18\frac{1}{2} \times 22$ in., 46×55 cm. Louvre, Paris

24 *Melting Snow at L'Estaque* (*Neige fondante à l'Estaque*), *c.* 1870. Oil on canvas, $28\frac{3}{4} \times 36\frac{1}{4}$ in., 73×92 cm. Bührle Collection, Zürich

25 *Flowers in a Delft Vase* (*Bouquet au petit Delft*), 1873–5. Oil on canvas, $16\frac{1}{8} \times 10\frac{5}{8}$ in., 41×27 cm. Louvre, Paris

26 *Glass and Apples* (*Verre et pommes*), 1879–82. Oil on canvas, $12\frac{1}{4} \times 15\frac{3}{4}$ in., 31×40 cm. Kunstmuseum, Basel

27 *The Suicide's House* (*La Maison du pendu, à Auvers*), 1872–3. Oil on canvas, $22\frac{1}{4} \times 26\frac{3}{4}$ in., $55{\cdot}5 \times 66{\cdot}5$ cm. Louvre, Paris

28 *Pissarro on His Way to Work* (*Pissarro allant peindre*), 1872–6. Pencil drawing, $7\frac{1}{4} \times 4\frac{1}{2}$ in., $19{\cdot}5 \times 11{\cdot}3$ cm. Louvre, Paris

29 *Auvers, Panoramic View* (*Auvers, vue panoramique*), 1873–5. Oil on canvas, $25\frac{1}{2} \times 31\frac{3}{4}$ in., 65×81 cm. Art Institute of Chicago

30 *The House of Dr Gachet, Auvers* (*La Maison du docteur Gachet, à Auvers*), 1873. Oil on canvas, $24\frac{7}{8} \times 20\frac{3}{4}$ in., 56×46 cm. Ryerson Collection, Chicago

31 *Crossroads at Auvers* (*Carrefour rue Rémy, à Auvers*), 1873. Oil on canvas, $15 \times 17\frac{7}{8}$ in., $38 \times 45{\cdot}5$ cm. Louvre, Paris

32 *The House of Père Lacroix, Auvers* (*La Maison du père Lacroix, à Auvers*), 1873. Oil on canvas, $24\frac{1}{2} \times 20$ in., $61{\cdot}5 \times 51$ cm. National Gallery of Art, Washington

33 *The Garden Gate* (*Entrée du jardin*), 1872–7. Water-colour, $18\frac{1}{8} \times 11\frac{3}{4}$ in., 46×30 cm. W. Weinberg Collection, Scarsdale, N.Y.

34 *L'Eternel Féminin*, 1875–7. Oil on canvas, $17 \times 20\frac{7}{8}$ in., 43×53 cm. Wildenstein Collection, New York

35 *Portrait of Cézanne's Father* (*Portrait du père de Cézanne*), 1878–9. Crayon, $8\frac{5}{8} \times 9\frac{7}{8}$ in., 22×25 cm. Collection of Mr and Mrs Emery Reves

36 *Bacchanal* (*La Lutte d'Amour*), 1875–80. Oil on canvas, $15 \times 18\frac{1}{8}$ in., 38×46 cm. Averell Harriman Collection, New York

37 *Portrait of Victor Chocquet* (*Portrait de Victor Chocquet*), 1875–7. Oil on canvas, $18\frac{1}{8} \times 14$ in., 46×36 cm. Private collection

38 *Madame Cézanne Sewing (Madame Cézanne cousant)*, c. 1877. Oil on canvas, $22\frac{7}{8} \times 18\frac{7}{8}$ in., 58×48 cm. Paul Rosenberg Collection, Paris

39 *Portrait of Madame Cézanne (Portrait de Madame Cézanne)*, 1879–82. Oil on canvas, $36\frac{3}{8} \times 28\frac{3}{4}$ in., $92 \cdot 5 \times 73$ cm. Bührle Collection, Zürich

40 *Trois Baigneuses*, 1879–82. Oil on canvas, $19\frac{5}{8} \times 19\frac{5}{8}$ in., 50×50 cm. Musée du Petit Palais, Paris

41 *Groupe de Baigneurs*, 1875–82. Water-colour. Private collection

42 *Trois Baigneuses*, 1872–7. Water-colour, $4\frac{3}{8} \times 5\frac{1}{8}$ in., 11×13 cm. Private collection

43 *Un Baigneur*, 1875–7. Oil on canvas, $12\frac{1}{4} \times 8\frac{1}{4}$ in., 31×21 cm. Joseph Mueller Collection, Soleure, Switzerland

44 *Self-portrait (Autoportrait)*, 1880–1. Oil on canvas. $10\frac{1}{4} \times 5\frac{7}{8}$ in., 26×15 cm. Louvre, Paris

45 *Still-life with Fruit (Nature morte aux fruits)*, 1879. Oil on canvas, $17\frac{3}{4} \times 21\frac{1}{4}$ in., 45×54 cm. Hermitage, Leningrad

46 *Mill on the Couleuvre at Pontoise (Moulin sur la Couleuvre, à Pontoise)*, 1879–82. Oil on canvas, $17\frac{3}{4} \times 20\frac{7}{8}$ in., 45×53 cm. National Gallery, East Berlin

47 *Poplars (Les Peupliers)*, 1879–82. Oil on canvas, $24\frac{3}{8} \times 30\frac{3}{4}$ in., 62×78 cm. Louvre, Paris

48 *La Côte du Galet, Pontoise*, 1879–82. Oil on canvas, $23\frac{3}{4} \times 28\frac{3}{4}$ in., 60×73 cm. Collection of Mrs Carroll S. Tyson, Philadelphia

49 *Self-portrait (Autoportrait)*, 1880–1. Oil on canvas, $22\frac{1}{2} \times 18\frac{1}{2}$ in., 57×47 cm. Private collection

50 *The Road and the Pond (La Route et l'étang)*, 1879–82. Oil on canvas, $31\frac{7}{8} \times 23\frac{5}{8}$ in., 81×60 cm. Rijksmuseum 'Kröller-Müller', Otterlo

51 *Le Château de Médan*, 1879–81. Oil on canvas, $23\frac{1}{4} \times 28\frac{3}{8}$ in., 59×72 cm. Glasgow Art Galleries and Museum, Glasgow

52 *The Little Bridge at Maincy (Le Pont de Maincy)*, c. 1882–5. Oil on canvas, $23\frac{5}{8} \times 28\frac{5}{8}$ in., 60×73 cm. Louvre, Paris

53 *The Bay of Marseilles Seen from L'Estaque (Le Golfe de Marseille, vu de l'Estaque)*, 1883–5. Oil on canvas, $22\frac{3}{4} \times 28\frac{1}{4}$ in., 58×72 cm. Louvre, Paris

54 *The Bay of Marseilles Seen from L'Estaque (Le Golfe de Marseille, vu de l'Estaque)*, 1883–5. Oil on canvas, $28\frac{3}{4} \times 39\frac{3}{8}$ in., 73×100 cm. Metropolitan Museum of Art, New York

55 *Rocks at L'Estaque (Rochers à l'Estaque)*, 1882–5. Oil on canvas, $28\frac{3}{4} \times 35\frac{3}{4}$ in., 73×91 cm. Museu de Arte, São Paulo

56 *The Chest of Drawers (Nature morte à la commode)*, 1883–7. Oil on canvas, $28 \times 35\frac{1}{2}$ in., 71×90 cm. Neue Staatsgalerie, Munich

57 *Still-life with Soup Tureen (Nature morte à la soupière)*, 1883–5. Oil on canvas, $25\frac{1}{2} \times 32$ in., 65×82 cm. Louvre, Paris

58 *The Kitchen Table (Nature morte au panier)*, 1888–90. Oil on canvas, $25\frac{1}{2} \times 32$ in., 65×81 cm. Louvre, Paris

59 *View of Gardanne (Gardanne)*, 1885–6. Oil on canvas, $36\frac{1}{4} \times 28\frac{3}{4}$ in., 92×73 cm. Brooklyn Museum, New York.

60 *Jas de Bouffan (Maison et ferme du Jas de Bouffan)*, 1885–7. Oil on canvas, $23\frac{3}{4} \times 28\frac{3}{4}$ in., 60 × 73 cm. National Gallery, Prague

61 *Self-portrait with Palette (Autoportrait à la palette)*, 1885–7. Oil on canvas, $36\frac{1}{4} \times 28\frac{3}{4}$ in., 92 × 73 cm. Bührle Collection, Zürich

62 *House on the Banks of the Marne (Maison au bord de la Marne)*, 1888–90. $25\frac{5}{8} \times 31\frac{7}{8}$ in., 65 × 81 cm. National Gallery of Art, Washington

63 *Dovecot at Bellevue (Pigeonnier à Bellevue)*, 1888–92. Oil on canvas, $25\frac{5}{8} \times 31\frac{7}{8}$ in., 65 × 81 cm. Cleveland Museum of Art

64 *Road at Chantilly (Allée à Chantilly)*, 1888. Oil on canvas, $31\frac{7}{8} \times 25\frac{5}{8}$ in., 81 × 65 cm. William A. Burden Collection, Washington

65 *Mountains in Provence (Montagnes en Provence)*, 1886–90. Oil on canvas, $21\frac{1}{4} \times 28\frac{3}{4}$ in., 54 × 73 cm. National Museum of Wales, Cardiff

66 *Little Paul (Le petit Paul)*, drawing, Musée du Petit Palais, Paris

67 *Chestnut Trees at the Jas de Bouffan (Marroniers du Jas de Bouffan)*, 1885–7. Oil on canvas, $28\frac{3}{4} \times 36\frac{1}{4}$ in., 73 × 92 cm. Minneapolis Institute of Arts

68 *Harlequin (Arlequin)*, preliminary sketch for *Mardi-Gras*, 1888. Drawing, $18\frac{1}{8} \times 10\frac{1}{4}$ in., 46 × 26 cm. Art Institute of Chicago

69 *Mardi-Gras*, 1888. Oil on canvas, $39\frac{3}{8} \times 31\frac{7}{8}$ in., 100 × 81 cm. Pushkin Museum, Moscow

70 *Portrait of Louis Guillaume (Portrait de Louis Guillaume)*, 1879–82. Oil on canvas, $22 \times 18\frac{1}{2}$ in., 56 × 47 cm. National Gallery of Art, Washington

71 *Still-life (Nature morte)*, 1888–90. Oil on canvas, $24 \times 35\frac{1}{2}$ in., 61 × 90 cm. Pushkin Museum, Moscow

72 *The Blue Vase (Le Vase bleu)*, 1883–7. Oil on canvas, $24\frac{1}{2} \times 20$ in., 61 × 50 cm. Louvre, Paris

73 *Still-life with Onions and Bottle (Oignons et bouteille)*, 1895–1900. $26 \times 32\frac{1}{4}$ in., 66 × 81 cm. Louvre, Paris

74 *The Stone Pitcher (Le Pichet de grès)*, 1885–7. Oil on canvas, $17 \times 24\frac{3}{4}$ in., 43 × 63 cm. Private collection

75 *Still-life with Cupid (L'Amour en plâtre)*, 1895. Oil on canvas, $24\frac{3}{4} \times 31\frac{7}{8}$ in., 63 × 81 cm. National Museum, Stockholm

76 *Vase of Tulips (Vase de tulipes)*, 1890–4. Oil on canvas, $23\frac{5}{8} \times 16\frac{1}{2}$ in., 60 × 42 cm. Art Institute of Chicago

77 *Woman with Coffee Pot (La Femme à la cafetière)*, 1890–4. Oil on canvas, $51\frac{1}{4} \times 38\frac{1}{4}$ in., 130 × 97 cm. Louvre, Paris

78 *Portrait of Ambroise Vollard (Portrait d'Ambroise Vollard)*, 1899. Oil on canvas, $39\frac{3}{8} \times 31\frac{7}{8}$ in., 100 × 81 cm. Musée du Petit Palais, Paris

79 *Boy in a Red Waistcoat (Garçon au gilet rouge)*, 1890–5. Oil on canvas, 31 × 25 in., 79 × 64 cm. Bührle Collection, Zürich

80 *Boy in a Red Waistcoat (Garçon au gilet rouge)*, 1890–5. Oil on canvas, 36 × 29 in., 92 × 73 cm. Paul Mellon Collection, Washington

81 *Portrait of Gustave Geffroy (Portrait de Gustave Geffroy)*, 1895. Oil on canvas, $45\frac{3}{8} \times 35$ in., 116 × 89 cm. Pellerin Collection, Paris

82 *The Young Italian Girl (Jeune Italienne accoudée)*, c. 1896. Oil on canvas, $45\frac{3}{8} \times 35$ in., 116 × 89 cm. Harry Bakwin Collection, New York

83 *Peasant (Le Paysan)*, 1890–2. Oil on canvas, 21⅝ × 18⅛ in., 55 × 46 cm. Hahnloser Collection, Winterthur

84 *Man with a Pipe (L'Homme à la pipe)*, 1890–4. Oil on canvas, 28¾ × 23½ in., 73 × 60 cm. Courtauld Institute, London

85 *The Card Players (Les Joueurs de cartes)*, 1890–2. Oil on canvas, 23½ × 28¾ in., 58 × 69 cm. Courtauld Institute, London

86 *The Card Players (Les Joueurs de cartes)*, 1890–2. Oil on canvas, 18½ × 22 in., 45 × 57 cm. Louvre, Paris

87 *The Card Players (Les Joueurs de cartes)*, 1890–2. Oil on canvas, 25⅝ × 31⅞ in., 65 × 81 cm. Metropolitan Museum of Art, New York

88 *The Card Player (Joueur de cartes)*, 1890–2. Pencil and water-colour. Museum of Fine Art, Providence, Rhode Island

89 *Great Pine at Mont Sainte-Victoire (La Montagne Sainte-Victoire au Grand Pin)*, 1885–7. Oil on canvas, 26 × 35⅝ in., 67 × 92 cm. Courtauld Institute, London

90 *Les Baigneurs,* 1890–4. Oil on canvas, 8½ × 13 in., 22 × 33 cm. Louvre, Paris

91 *Madame Cézanne in the Conservatory (Madame Cézanne dans la serre)*, c. 1890. Oil on canvas, 36¼ × 28¾ in., 92 × 73 cm. Stephen C. Clark Collection, New York

92 *Madame Cézanne,* 1890–4. Oil on canvas, 35½ × 27½ in., 91 × 70 cm. Museu de Arte, São Paulo

93 *Self-portrait (Autoportrait)*, 1890–4. Oil on canvas, 18⅛ × 15¾ in., 46 × 40 cm. Pellerin Collection, Paris

94 *Cézanne in a Soft Hat (Autoportrait au chapeau mou)*, 1890–4. Oil on canvas, Ishibashi Collection, Tokyo

95 *Leda and the Swan (Leda au cygne)*, 1886–90. Oil on canvas, 23⅝ × 28¾ in., 60 × 73 cm. Pellerin Collection, Paris

96 *Sainte-Victoire,* 1896. Water-colour, Courtauld Institute, London

97 *Portrait of Joachim Gasquet (Portrait de Joachim Gasquet)*, c. 1896–7. Oil on canvas, 25⅝ × 21¼ in., 65 × 54 cm. National Gallery, Prague

98 *The Lake of Annecy (Lac d'Annecy)*, 1896. Oil on canvas, 25½ × 32 in., 64 × 79 cm. Courtauld Institute, London

99 *Rocks in a Wood (Rochers dans le bois),* 1894–8. Oil on canvas, 28¾ × 36¼ in., 48·5 × 59·5 cm. Kunsthaus, Zürich

100 *Rocks at Fontainebleau (Rochers à Fontainebleau)*, 1894–8. Oil on canvas, 28¾ × 36¼ in., 73 × 92 cm. Metropolitan Museum of Art, New York

101 *Rocks and Trees at Bibémus (Rochers et branches à Bibémus)*, 1900–4. Oil on canvas, 19⅝ × 24 in., 50 × 61 cm. Musée du Petit Palais, Paris

102 *Seated Man (Homme assis)*, c. 1898–1900. Oil on canvas, 39⅜ × 28¾ in., 100 × 73 cm. National Gallery, Oslo

103 *Still-life with Curtain (Nature morte au rideau)*, 1895–1900. Oil on canvas, 20½ × 28⅜ in., 52 × 72 cm. Hermitage, Leningrad

104 *Still life with Fruit (Fruits sur un linge)*, 1890–4. Oil on canvas, Ishibashi Collection, Tokyo

105 *Still-life with Skull and Candlestick* (*Nature morte au crâne et au chandelier*), *c.* 1900. Oil on canvas, 24 × 19⅝ in., 61 × 50 cm. Staatsgalerie, Stuttgart

106 Maurice Denis, *Homage to Cézanne* (*Hommage à Cézanne*), detail, 1900. Oil on canvas, 68⅞ × 94½ in., 180 × 240 cm. Musée Nationale d'Art Moderne, Paris

107 *Forest Landscape* (*La Forêt: sous-bois*), 1892–4. Oil on canvas, 36¼ × 29⅛ in., 92 × 74 cm. National Gallery of Art, Washington

108 *Pine-tree near Aix* (*Le Grand Pin et les terres rouges*), 1885–7. Oil on canvas, 28⅜ × 35⅞ in., 72 × 91 cm. Pushkin Museum, Moscow

109 *The Millstone* (*La Meule*), 1898–1900. Oil on canvas, 28¾ × 36¼ in., 73 × 92 cm. Collection of Mrs Carroll S. Tyson, Philadelphia

110 *Mont Sainte-Victoire Seen from Bibémus* (*La Montagne Sainte-Victoire, vue de Bibémus*), 1898–1900. Oil on canvas, 25⅝ × 31⅞ in., 65 × 81 cm. Baltimore Museum of Art

111 *The House with Cracked Walls* (*La Maison lézardée*), *c.* 1896. Oil on canvas, 25⅝ × 21¼ in., 65 × 54 cm. Collection of Mr and Mrs Ira P. Haupt, New York

112 *Mont Sainte-Victoire and the Château Noir* (*La Montagne Sainte-Victoire et le Château Noir*), 1898–1900. Oil on canvas, Ishibashi Collection, Tokyo

113 *Le Château Noir*, 1904–6. Oil on canvas, 28¾ × 36¼ in., 73 × 92 cm. Collection of Mrs David M. Levy, New York

114 *Mountain Stream* (*Au Fond du ravin*), 1882–5. Oil on canvas, 28¾ × 21¼ in., 73 × 54 cm. Joseph Mueller Collection, Soleure, Switzerland

115 *Farm in Normandy: The Orchard* (*Ferme en Normandie: le verger*), 1885–6. Oil on canvas, 25⅝ × 31⅞ in., 65 × 81 cm. Collection of the Marquise de Ganay, Paris

116 *Self-portrait with Béret* (*Autoportrait au béret basque*), 1898–1900. Oil on canvas, 25⅝ × 21¼ in., 65 × 54 cm. Robert Treat Paine Collection, Boston

117 *Man with a Pipe* (*Le Fumeur*), *c.* 1895–1900. Oil on canvas, 36 × 28½ in., 91 × 72 cm. Pushkin Museum, Moscow

118 *Head of an Old man* (*Tête de vieillard*), 1860–5. Oil on canvas, 20 × 19 in., 51 × 48 cm. Louvre, Paris

119 *La Colline des Pauvres*, 1888–94. Oil on canvas, 25⅝ × 31⅞ in., 65 × 81 cm. Metropolitan Museum of Art, New York

120 *The Viaduct* (*Le Viaduc*), 1898–1902. Oil on canvas, 36 × 28 in., 91 × 71 cm. Pushkin Museum, Moscow

121 *Bridge and Pool* (*Le Pont sur l'étang*), 1888–90. Oil on canvas, 25¼ × 31⅛ in., 64 × 79 cm. Pushkin Museum, Moscow

122 *Mont Sainte-Victoire* (*La Montagne Sainte-Victoire*), 1900–6. Oil on canvas, 23⅝ × 28¾ in., 60 × 73 cm. Pushkin Museum, Moscow

123 *The Gardener* (*Le Jardinier*), 1900–6. Oil on canvas, 24¾ × 20½ in., 63 × 52 cm. Tate Gallery, London

124 *Mont Sainte-Victoire* (*La Montagne Sainte-Victoire*), 1904–6. Oil on canvas, 25⅝ × 31⅞ in., 65 × 81 cm. Kunsthaus, Zürich

125 *Sainte-Victoire*, 1905–6. Oil on canvas, $28\frac{3}{4}$ × $36\frac{1}{4}$ in., 73 × 92 cm. Philadelphia Museum of Art

126 *Sainte-Victoire,* 1904–6. Oil on canvas, $21\frac{1}{4}$ × $28\frac{3}{4}$ in., 54 × 73 cm. Galerie Beyeler, Basel

127 *Portrait of Vallier (Portrait de Vallier)*, 1906. Oil on canvas, $25\frac{5}{8}$ × $21\frac{1}{4}$ in., 65 × 54 cm. Leigh Block Collection, Chicago

128 *The Watchmaker (L'Horloger)*, 1895–1900. Oil on canvas, $36\frac{1}{4}$ × $28\frac{3}{4}$ in., 92 × 73 cm. Guggenheim Museum, New York

129 *Woman in a Hat (Femme au chapeau)*, 1900–4. Oil on canvas, $25\frac{5}{8}$ × $19\frac{3}{4}$ in., 65 × 50 cm. Wildenstein Collection, New York

130 *Old Woman with Rosary (Vieille au chapelet)*, 1900–4. Oil on canvas, $33\frac{1}{2}$ × $25\frac{5}{8}$ in., 85 × 65 cm. National Gallery, London

131 *Peasant (Paysan)*, 1895–1900. Oil on canvas, $31\frac{7}{8}$ × $25\frac{5}{8}$ in., 81 × 65 cm. A. Conger Goodyear Collection, New York

132 *Still-life with Apples and Oranges (Pommes et oranges)*, 1895–1900. Oil on canvas, $28\frac{5}{8}$ × $36\frac{1}{2}$ in., 73 × 92 cm. Louvre, Paris

133 *Still-life with Apples (Nature morte aux pommes)*, 1895–1900. Oil on canvas, $26\frac{3}{4}$ × $36\frac{1}{4}$ in., 68 × 92 cm. Museum of Modern Art, New York

134 *The Great Pine (Le Grand Pin)*, 1892–6. Oil on Canvas, $33\frac{1}{2}$ × $36\frac{1}{4}$ in., 85 × 92 cm. Museu de Arte, São Paulo

135 *View of the Château Noir (Vue du Château Noir)*, 1894–6. Oil on canvas, $28\frac{3}{4}$ × $36\frac{1}{4}$ in., 73 × 92 cm. Oskar Reinhart Collection, Winterthur

136 *Montgeroult at Sunset (Montgeroult au couchant)*, 1899. Oil on canvas, $25\frac{1}{2}$ × $20\frac{1}{2}$ in., 81 × 65 cm. John Hay Whitney Collection, New York

137 *Le Cabanon de Jourdan*, 1906. Oil on canvas, $25\frac{5}{8}$ × $31\frac{7}{8}$ in., 65 × 81 cm. Collection of Dr Jucke, Milan

138 *Le Grand Baigneur*, 1885–7. Oil on canvas, 50 × $38\frac{1}{2}$ in., 126 × 95 cm. Museum of Modern Art, New York

139 *Les Grandes Baigneuses*, 1898–1905. Oil on canvas, 82 × 98 in., 208 × 249 cm. Philadelphia Museum of Art

140 *Baigneurs,* 1890–1900. Lithograph, 9 × 11 in., 23 × 28 cm. Barnes Foundation, Merion, Pennsylvania

141 Cézanne with *Les Grandes Baigneuses*

142 *Still-life (Nature morte), c.* 1900. Water-colour, $18\frac{7}{8}$ × $24\frac{3}{8}$ in., 48 × 62 cm. Collection of Mr and Mrs Emery Reves

143 *Boy in a Red Waistcoat (Garçon au gilet rouge)*, 1890–5. Water-colour drawing. Feilchenfeld Collection, Zürich

144 *Female Nude (Femme nu), c.* 1895. Pencil, water-colour and pastel, 35 × $20\frac{7}{8}$ in., 89 × 53 cm. Formerly in the collection of Ambroise Vollard

145 *Mont Sainte-Victoire (Montagne Sainte-Victoire)*, 1883–7. Water-colour, $13\frac{3}{8}$ × $20\frac{1}{2}$ in., 34 × 52 cm. Formerly in the collection of Cézanne's son

146 *The Dessert (Le Dessert)*, 1900–6. Water-colour, $18\frac{1}{2}$ × 24 in., 47 × 61 cm. Gaston Bernheim de Villiers Collection, Paris

147 *The Pitcher (Le Cruchon)*, 1885–95. Water-colour, $7\frac{5}{8}$ × $9\frac{1}{8}$ in., 19·5 × 23·2 cm. Louvre, Paris

Index

Photographic sources

Bernheim: pls. 1, 7, 11, 12, 13, 21, 31, 33, 38, 42, 43, 49, 74, 81, 93, 96, 109, 114, 140, 149, 151, 155, 156, 162; Bulloz: pls. 3, 5, 6, 10, 22, 34, 39, 46, 48, 66, 84, 88, 89, 95, 120, 131, 145; Editions Cercle d'Art: pls. 45, 71, 103, 108, 117, 121, 122; Giraudon: pls. 2, 14, 15, 18, 20, 28, 40, 47, 55, 60, 65, 68, 73, 78, 79, 85, 90, 92, 94, 97, 98, 99, 104, 106, 107, 110, 112, 115, 118, 119, 124, 128, 132, 133, 143, 148, 160; Hinz: pls. 8, 26, 61, 83, 126, 135, 137; Service Photographique des Musées Nationaux, Versailles: pls. 144, 146, 147, 150, 152, 153, 154, 157, 158, 159; Sirot: pl. 141; Roger-Viollet: pls. 161, 163.